Wider Horizons:
Naval Policy & International Affairs

The third & last book of a trilogy
"Admiral Jim"

Other books of the trilogy

Book 1   "From Greenland's Icy Shore"

Book 2   "Life on the Ocean Wave"

Wider Horizons:
Naval Policy &
International Affairs

by
Admiral Sir James Eberle
GCB LLD

Copyright © 2007 Admiral Sir James Eberle

All rights reserved. No part of this publication may be reproduced, stored in a retrieval system, or transmitted in any form or by any means without the prior written permission of the author and publisher, nor be otherwise circulated in any form of binding or cover other than that in which it is published and without a similar condition including this condition being imposed on the subsequent purchaser.

ISBN 978-1-904499-17-6

Further copies of this book may be obtained from
jimeberle@btinternet.com

First published in United Kingdom of Great Britain in 2007 by
Roundtuit Publishing, 32 Cookes Wood, Broompark, Durham DH7 7RL

Cover image – Dawn over the Atlantic 2007 by N. Radford

Printed in the United Kingdom of Great Britain by Prontaprint Durham

Preface to the Trilogy
"Admiral Jim"

I am not sure when the urge first came to me to write an account of my own personal journey through life. I only know that, as my active life has started to draw to a close, I have became more and more aware of the variety and nature of events in which I have been personally involved – from World War II, the Korean War, the South Atlantic War, the Cold War, and the Cold Peace that followed it, to the 'War on Terror'. All too often when I had been speaking to friends and colleagues about some particular events they had responded 'Oh, you must write all this down'. Indeed, in some cases, these events may not have been previously recorded at all, and may well be of interest to modern political, military and social historians.

However, I had long before been aware that my ancestors had also had very interesting lives about which I knew little and understood less. I believed the Eberle family to be quintessentially English and Bristolian. Indeed, I had at an early age been privileged to become a Freeman of that city. I was vaguely aware that the family had a Moravian connection but I did not really know where Moravia was or how it fitted in to our family history.

Shortly before he died in 1987, my father handed to me a copy of a brief treatise that he had written, entitled "The Eberle Family History". With it, I inherited a considerable mass of ancient books, documents and family papers. Included in those papers was a treatise entitled "The Eberles" written by an American cousin. Engrossed as I was at that time in the very good fortunes of my own life, I gave these papers not more than a cursory glance, and put them aside to be studied in due course. It is only recently that the pace of my life has slowed sufficiently to allow me to look at them more closely.

I soon discovered that my great grandfather was not British at all – he was German, and he had spent very little time in Bristol. The more I delved, the more I became confused. The story that I was trying to unravel seemed to represent a fascinating multi-faceted but incomplete picture of my family's past – of which I had had neither the knowledge nor the understanding to appreciate. I was inspired however by my father's brief preface to his work in which he wrote:

> "This is a short record of what we know about the families from whom you and I are directly descended. Some day you may wish to read more about them from the original memoirs and other recorded facts, which have been handed down to us. I hope that you will feel proud in the knowledge that members of our family have lived strenuous and useful lives, in which, by their own unselfish labours, they strove to bring happiness to others. Our story shows, too, in generation after generation, a readiness to accept adventure and responsibility, and to face dangers and difficulties with courage and resolution. There is another reason why I wanted you to know more about those from whom you are descended. It is a proven fact that particular gifts and traits of character are handed on from one generation to another. From this you may learn that you have received a heritage that should encourage in you a similar strength of character and belief in the Christian religion and way of life. May this strengthen you in you determination to be worthy of that heritage in your own life."

These words clearly reflected not only his own personal experiences in the First World War throughout the four years of which he served in France and Italy in the Royal Engineers, which he recorded in his book "My Sapper Venture" published in 1973, but also suggested an earlier and 'deeper' history of the Eberle family.

As I delved through the family papers, I became increasingly aware that there were a number of detailed and fascinating accounts of events involving the family dating back to the seventeenth century and beyond. The more I found out, the more I wanted to know; and the more apparent it became that I must undertake a short pilgrimage to both Germany and Greenland, if I was to be able to answer the many questions that were flooding through my mind.

At that time there was an opportunity. My son was retiring from the Navy and, in October 2005, we were both able to find the inside of a week in which we could visit the places in Germany where our family had lived to see if we could learn and understand more of our early family history. With the enthusiastic and invaluable support of my son, a fluent German speaker, we enlisted assistance from wherever we could find it. This pilgrimage, about which I have already written, was an unqualified and outstanding success. I learnt more and understood more than I could possibly have expected. It was full of fascinating discoveries; and those extraordinary coincidences that seem regularly to have punctuated my life.

Most fascinating of all was to learn that the Moravian Church called on all its members to write down in their later years a story of their life – their "Lebenslauf". These accounts are carefully preserved, many of them in the archives at the Moravian settlement at Herrnhut. The story that these tell is totally fascinating and absorbing and includes a period of over one hundred years that my forbears spent in Greenland as missionaries of the Moravian Church. I returned to England determined that I must also visit Greenland. This my son and I achieved in the summer of 2006.

As I started to write, I came to realise that the story that I had to tell was not just an autobiography, but was in turn, an episode of social history stretching back for three hundred years; a light hearted account of life in the Royal Navy from the final days of World War II, from hot war to cold peace; and the later stages of a career in which I found myself closely involved at a high level in international diplomacy.

JE

Homestead Farm,
North Houghton,
Stockbridge,
Hampshire,
SO20 6LG

Admiral Jim: A Trilogy
Book 3
Wider Horizons: Naval Policy & International Diplomacy

This book, the third of Admiral Jim's trilogy, describes in personal terms the years following a seagoing career as it moves from the sphere of men and the machinery of war to the experience of the highest levels of naval command and then of international diplomacy.

The previous two books were...

Book 1–From Greenland's Icy Shore. This is the story of the Eberle family's origin in Germany in the political and religious turmoil of the seventeenth century, the founding of the Moravian church and the growing commitment to it of the lives of my ancestors. Their adventures over one hundred years of Moravian missionary work in Greenland; their emigration from Germany and their absorption into British and American society, leading in England to prominence in civic affairs in both countries. This is social history.

Book 2–Life on the Ocean Wave provides a light-hearted account of life in the Navy after the final days of WW II – from hot war to cold peace. This was the period of Britain's withdrawal from Empire and gradual decline as a global power. It is seen through the eyes of a young Naval Officer who was fortunate in later having had a very varied and interesting career, and in receiving very early promotion to Flag Rank.

Book 3 begins with his appointment to the Admiralty Board and his final two appointments, firstly as Commander-in-Chief Fleet and secondly Commander-in-Chief Home Command. Commander-in-Chief Fleet carried with it a number of other appointments, the principal of which were the NATO Commander-in-Chief Channel Command and NATO Commander-in-Chief Eastern Atlantic. He retired from the Navy in 1983, having served for eleven years as an Admiral.

His subsequent life became closely associated with the world of international politics. He was appointed Director of the Royal

Institute of International Affairs at Chatham House, an internationally respected think-tank that had been established in the immediate aftermath of WWI. He himself describes it as "a think-tank before think-tanks were thought of".

As Director of the Royal Institute he was closely linked to the events that led to and followed the collapse of Soviet communism. He established strong contacts with Moscow and in Chapter 6 relates some of the high level non-governmental exchanges that accompanied those events

He was also able to make the first informal contacts with Buenos Aires following the long period of stand-off between Britain and Argentina that followed the ending of the Falkland Islands war. In 1n 1989, he was the first senior Briton to establish contact with the new Menim Government.

He also became closely involved both in Britain's growing relationship with Japan and in other developments in South East Asia.

His final chapter is a personal assessment of the international security situation following the disastrous events of the Iraqi war and the impact of operations in Afghanistan. He looks forward to the prospects for meeting the wider global challenge of religious fundamentalism, associated with the war on terrorism.

Table of Contents

Wider Horizons:
Naval Policy & International Affairs

1– The Board of Admiralty.. 1
2– National and NATO Commander-in-Chief................ 16
3– Commander-in-Chief, Naval Home Command........ 40
4– The Royal Institute of International Affairs 58
5– Europe...84
6– Moscow and the Soviet Union 101
7– Argentina and the Falkland Islands 126
8– The Asia Pacific Region.. 135
9– The 21st Century, Terrorism and the Future 152
Epilogue 171
The Author.. 172

Acknowledgments

I'm telling this story without ever having kept a diary. I have been astonished, however, at my ability to recall events of long ago that must have lain dormant in my mind for many years. Where others may find me in error, I apologise.

On more recent events, I am most grateful to many friends who have offered their comments and advice. Where there are still mistakes, the fault remains my own.

I could not have completed this work without the most admirable help of Delia Merison in its presentation.

The Navy ~Board in the Admiralty Board Room, Whitehall

Chapter 1

The Board of Admiralty

"Today, I had my first Cabinet meeting as Prime Minister. I gave them their orders and they wanted to stay and discuss them."
Field Marshal, the Duke of Wellington, 1903

With my appointment as a member of the Admiralty Board and Chief of Fleet Support (CFS) I appreciated that I was starting at the beginning of a new chapter in my life. As described in Book 2, most of my naval career was principally associated with sailors, their equipment and the military challenges of the post Second World War era. I had interested myself particularly during my time at Oxford, undertaking my defence fellowship, in the interrelationship of political and military factors in the conduct of operations. I was now entering a field where I would become involved in the interaction of political and military factors concerned with major aspects of defence policy.

The Board of Admiralty has a long history. From 1628 until 1964, the Board of Admiralty "executed the Office of the Lord High Admiral". The office of the Lord High Admiral was first held by the sovereign, then Charles II, in 1660. In 1689, the sovereign established a new Board of Admiralty under Admiral Arthur Herbert as First Lord of the Admiralty. Samuel Pepys was nominated as Secretary of the Admiralty. In 1964, the Board of Admiralty, the Army Board and the Air Force Board were brought by Act of Parliament under the control of a newly formed Defence Council.

Parliament also attempted to abolish the titles of the Sea Lords who formed the naval members of the new Admiralty Board. However, a spirited defence in parliament succeeded in maintaining the traditional title of the Navy's most senior serving admiral as First Sea Lord. The title of Second Sea Lord (who was chief of naval personnel) was also rescued on the basis that you could not have a First Sea Lord unless there was a Second Sea,

Defense and Navy Board Members afloat

Lord. The title of Third Sea Lord was changed to that of the Controller of the Navy and the Fourth Sea Lord became the Chief of Fleet Support. The Vice Chief of the Naval Staff retained his title. The Board of Admiralty became the Navy Board of the Defence Council, which sat under the chairmanship of the Navy Minister (the Under Secretary of State for the Royal Navy), who was himself a member of the Defence Council.

As I attempted to understand the responsibilities of a member of the Admiralty Board I found myself unclear as to the degree to which each board member bore personal responsibility for all the decisions of the board. I clearly recognised my full responsibility for all those matters pertaining to my new appointment as Chief of Fleet Support. But what about the matters which were the full responsibility of other members of the board? Did I carry a measure of responsibility for their decisions also? The answer never became entirely clear to me. In practical terms each board member would formally approve a decision by his signature at the end of a docket in which a policy had been proposed and which had attracted the comments of other departments belonging to other board members.

In practical terms the conduct of formal meetings of the Admiralty Board did not encourage a sense of corporate responsibility. We conducted our board meetings in the traditional Admiralty Board room in the old Admiralty building in Whitehall. This is one of the least well known of the historic rooms in London. The Navy Minister at this time was Patrick Duffy, a socialist of the old order, whom I liked and respected. However, under his chairmanship our meetings might well have been described as meetings of the bored. An item on the agenda, which had essentially already been agreed, was first commented on by the responsible board member. The minister then went round the table in order. "Second Sea Lord, what do you think about this?" He was then expected to give a short response. "Controller, what do you think about this?" and so on round the table until it got to the First Sea Lord who would also give a brief view. There was seldom, if ever, an opportunity for dialogue or for weighing the pros and cons and very rarely any substantive discussion. The minister would then say "approved". Apparently this was the way that Mrs Thatcher ran her cabinet. She would have, wouldn't she?

The result of this so-called traditional practice meant that the real business of discussion at board level occurred at meetings of the five naval members of the board. They were known as NAVIs. They were entirely informal. They were led by the First Sea Lord, always referred to as 'First'. He was Terry Lewin, an outstanding leader and man of great substance. The Vice Chief, responsible for the shape and size of the future fleet (the 'ops man') was Tony Moreton. The Second Sea Lord, the chief of naval personnel (the 'man man') was Gordon Tait, a New Zealander of great personality, ideally suited to this task. The Controller of the Navy, who was responsible for the procurement of naval ships and weapons (the 'thing man') was Dick Clayton. The Chief of Fleet Support responsible for naval support and logistics (the 'log man') was myself. In more recent times, the membership of the board has been widened to include the Commander-in-Chief Fleet. The Commander-in-Chief Naval Home Command has also been merged with the Chief of Naval Personnel. The Board now meets with the First Sea Lord in the chair, and is known as the Navy Board.

In our board, we all got on extremely well at every level, which had not always happened in the past. Although it may well be claimed that conflict sharpens the process of decision-making, I have no doubt that the Navy benefits more from harmony. Our discussions could nonetheless be vigorous. It was certainly so in regard to issues of the defence budget. 'First' was strongly of the view that the forward deployment in Germany of so much of the British Army, which was extremely costly, was more of a carry-over from the Second World War than a necessary contribution to NATO's cold war stance. He was anxious to raise the issue informally in the Chief's staff committee. The rest of us did not agree with this, as we were concerned that the army might retaliate with challenging some of our own material budget; or seek to take over the Royal Marines.

Furthermore, there was no longer adequate space in the UK for the Rhine Army is accommodation and training. Thus, it was better to let sleeping dogs lie. In hindsight we were probably both right – but 4-1 won the day. The issue was to re-appear however in the 1981 (Nott) Defence Review.

The other issue that concerned us deeply was that the rising overall cost of the defence budget might put at risk the Navy's aircraft carrier programme, a situation that we had faced before in 1966. Terry Lewin asked our view on whether, in the event that the carriers were about to be axed on financial grounds, his fellow board members believed that this should be a resigning issue. Our advice was that we did not think the resignation of the First Sea Lord would reverse such a decision – but if, nevertheless, the First Sea Lord thought otherwise, then we the other naval board members would also resign en bloc. These issues were also to raise their head during the 1981 Defence Review.

Resignation by any member of the board carried with it serious personal implications – in that it risked the loss of pension rights. But what if, in a very serious clash between the military and the government over security policy, the board collectively elected to resign their commissions prematurely? I don't know the answer.

The Chiefs-of-Staff Committee had similar problems in the matter of the proper forum for the resolution of conflicting inter-service issues. The Defence Council, chaired by the Secretary of State for Defence, was far too large and unwieldy to be an effective policy-making body. The three chiefs-of-staff therefore also met informally so as to provide a forum for tri-service issues. These meetings were known as COSIs.

The annual defence budgeting process, known as the long term costing (LTC), was itself, in my view, a nightmare. It ranged over a ten-year period of which the last six years were little more than a wish list. The big projects, all of them big spenders, could well extend over many years for the development, production and hand-over to the military. The first four years were the more important. The first part of the process was the publication of the LTC assumptions, which were the work of the joint planners. The spend for the first year formed the basis of the next year's budget. Using the LTC assumptions, departments did their costings in great detail. These were then scrutinized by their responsible naval board member. When the numbers were all added up, they were always over the top of what had been provisionally allocated. But 'shadow cuts' were available to save the day.

The shadow cut was recognition of past experience in which it was easily demonstrated that the actual spend in the next year was consistently under budget. Since Treasury rules then forbade any carry-over into the following financial year any money under spent was money lost to the Treasury. This seemed a sensible way of recognising reality – but when the shadow cut came to a figure of almost twenty percent, it made the budgeting process something of a farce. One was pressing departments to be as realistic as possible in their projected spend – and then, on no evidence other than of a historical nature, you had to tell them that they must be satisfied with four-fifths of what they had carefully calculated as their minimum cash requirement.

Another major weakness was the result of the Treasury's refusal to agree to any carry-over. Thus as the financial year drew to a close at the end of March, the estimate of out-turn led to a load of nonsense. If an under-spend appeared likely, then one had money to spare. But what could you spend it on which would bring in the bills to be paid before the first of April? The answer of course was not very much. The popular solution for the Navy was oil fuel. But then you had to be sure that you had tanks to store it in. As an ultimate last resort on over-spend you postponed paying bills until after the turn of the financial year. I am assured that things now are much better but I suspect relations with the Treasury still remain very difficult.

The defence budgeting process was strictly under the overall control of the civil service in the Ministry of Defence. For major items in the budget, even when it had overall approval, the spend had to be cleared with the Treasury who inevitably came up with questions. The big game was how to respond. Personally I thought that their questions were, on the whole, of a reasonable character. Nevertheless, they drove the service officers of the Ministry of Defence, if not the secretariat, mad. Nearly all these efforts went into obfuscating the issue. My own view was that in general they should get a reasonable answer – even if that answer could not be clear-cut. The tendency of senior uniformed officers wanting to tell the truth was held to be extremely dangerous. There was therefore a strict embargo on any senior service officer corresponding directly with the Treasury. I thought this a great pity but in this instance was on a loser. I was fortunate however in having an Assistant Under Secretary who was one of the few people in Whitehall who really understood government finance. He was of great help to me in telling the situation as it was, even though the situation was difficult.

Relationships with parliament were on a similar basis. Within the Ministry of Defence I was one of only two serving officers who were formally responsible direct to parliament for their budgets - the CFS and the director of Royal Ordnance factories. We were accountable through the Public Accounts Committee (PAC) of parliament, which was viewed by most civil servants to be of a nature that could only be compared with the Star Chamber. The accounting officers' personal fortune was at risk for any mishandling in his department - I would have been delighted to hand over my overdraft.

I was only once summoned by the PAC. The issue related to the purchase from Sweden of a tug which was required for special duties in the Clyde, connected with the deployment of the nuclear deterrent. In short we bought 'a pig in a poke'. The purchase also involved the Procurement Agency of the Ministry of Defence. The Chief of Defence Procurement (CDP), Sir Cliff Cawnford, led on this matter. I lost count of the number of briefings within the Ministry of Defence that he and I had on the issue. Come the day we did not escape all criticism, nor should we have, but in the view of some we got away with it. On its conclusion I remember commenting to CDP, "If your department and mine had put as much effort into getting this matter right in the first place, as we have done in trying to explain why it went wrong and why it was not our fault, we would all have been much better off."

At a similar level there was much reluctance to service officers appearing before the Parliamentary Defence Committee. As Chief of Fleet Support, my primary problem was the overrun in cost and time of the refitting of the ships of the fleet within the naval dockyards. In my view it was not unreasonable for the Defence Committee to call for an enquiry on these continuing cost and time overruns and to require my formal appearance before them. This caused deep concern in some sections of my department. I shared their concern as to the problem, which was very real and difficult. But I was perfectly prepared to tell it as it was to the Defence Committee. My Civil Service advisors were, however, opposed to this proposition. The problems were so complex that obfuscation would have been easy. I was not prepared to obfuscate. In the event, I quite enjoyed my appearance before the committee and concluded that they appreciated the opportunity to understand why it was all very difficult. When I returned to my office and reported the summing up of the committee chairman, to which I had no objections, my staff wondered how the hell I'd got away with it. Such was life in learning the ways of Whitehall and Westminster.

The support of the fleet, both ashore and afloat, was a very large multi-faceted task involving both uniformed and civilian labour. Shoreside support was centred around four principal naval bases at Rosyth, Chatham, Portsmouth and Devonport. There was also a naval base at Faslane which was the support and operational base for nuclear powered submarines – although docking and refitting facilities for SS(N)'s were available at Rosyth, Chatham and Devonport. Each of the four naval bases was under the charge of a Port Admiral. Within the base there was a royal dockyard that carried out the major and short refits of all surface ships and conventionally powered submarines. There was an additional dockyard at Gibraltar. The dockyards were functionally responsible to a Chief Executive (CED) whose department, situated in Bath, was under my direction. The department had a staff of at least six hundred people.

Within the naval base structure were the supply depots for the fuel, ammunition, naval and victualling stores of the Royal Naval Stores and Transport Service (RNSTS). They were functionally responsible to the Director General, Naval Stores and Transport whose department was also situated in Bath. Under his control were a number of shore-side supply depots situated at various locations around the country. Additionally, he was responsible for the management of the Navy's considerable force of supply ships and tankers, the Royal Fleet Auxiliary (RFA), which provided the afloat support for the operational fleet. With a seemingly ever increasing 'out of area' deployment for ships of the fleet, the tanker fleet was normally at full stretch. They were dedicated and very efficient. During my watch as CFS we carried out a major review of the future logistic requirements of the fleet, which resulted in the building of a new class of large tankers and large one-stop supply ships. Previously, supply ships had been dedicated either to ammunition, general stores or air stores. In the development of these ideas, which included the ability to operate anti-submarine helicopters and to be fitted with a defensive armament, we had to consider carefully the degree to which they would remain classified in international law as merchant ships, or would have to be reclassified as war ships. Today, many of the RFA ships are fitted with self-defence weapons. The RFA now has a fleet of nineteen ships, two fast fleet tankers, four fleet support tankers, two small fleet tankers, four replenishment ships, four landing ship (dock) auxiliaries, one landing ship logistic, one forward repair ship and one aviation training/casualty receiving ship.

Within the naval bases were also a uniformed Fleet Maintenance Group (FMG), a Port Auxiliary Service (PAS) to provide tugs and harbour transportation facilities, and a Queen's Harbour Master (QHM) who controlled all ship movements within the port. Additionally, and also under the Assistant Chief of Fleet Support, was the Naval Air Repair Organisation and the naval works programme in which the Director of Quartering was working hard to improve shore side accommodation standards[1].

The problem with the royal dockyards which carried out the refits and modernisation of our ships was indeed complex. When a refit or modernisation badly overran the cost or time estimates, it was extremely difficult to discern whether the overrun had been due to bad estimating or bad work control. We were also working in an almost continual climate of threatened industrial action. There was a feeling in the fleet that the dockyards worked to their own time rather than to meet a set target. The graffiti that I saw painted on the steel bulkhead of a ship in dockyard hands read, "Don't weld here – wait for overtime". That said it all.

To what extent the blame lay with senior management, or at lower levels of management at the workface, was also extremely difficult to ascertain. At the most senior levels, management in the royal dockyards was in the hands of the Naval Corps of Naval Constructors. The corps formed the very bedrock of naval experience in ship design and construction. However, they received no formal training in management, a weakness that was often evident, especially in comparison with conditions where senior management was in the hands of uniformed naval officers, such as in the Naval Air Repair Organisation; although industrial action there was not unknown.

The workforce in the dockyards was divided in accordance with civil service principles between the non-industrials, which included the supervisory grades, and the industrials. They had a differing union structure which tended to make this artificial differentiation the more frustrating both for the workforce and for management. In preparing the annual load-capacity balance, the load almost always exceeding the capacity. This raised the question as to whether the balance might be struck by increasing the supervision and thus better management; or increasing the industrial workforce. These were questions which we were consistently unable to answer in any meaningfully structured way.

---

[1] *See Book 2, Chapter 12*

It could only be a matter of judgment – and we didn't always get this right.

Although the management of the Whitley process that governed the way that the government dealt with the unions was in civilian hands within my department, it was inevitable that I, at the most senior level, had a part to play. The union leaders were, I found, seldom totally unreasonable – but it was their task to back the interests of their members. Government ministers were almost totally beholden to the union leaders and would very seldom approve any steps that might be seen as putting penalties on the unions for poor performance. It was like trying to fight with one hand tied behind one's back. We made some limited progress in putting some refitting work out to contract with civilian yards but opportunities were limited. At the senior level in the naval dockyard ports, the almost complete absence of effective sanctions for poor performance in meeting agreed targets was the cause of great frustration.

Three incidents come to my mind. The first was at Gibraltar where the Transport and General Workers Union were the dominant union throughout the dockyard. My first engagement on arrival at the dockyard was a meeting with the head of the T&GWU. He was an industrial worker, Joe Bessano. He had the reputation of being militant. He later became Chief Minister in the local government of Gibraltar. I was in full workday naval uniform. He walked in to the office wearing his workday uniform – turned-down sea boots and a leather jacket. I got the message. Nevertheless, he was a man that I found I could do business with. The dockyard was complaining that they were not getting sufficient work put in to the yard. Their output performance had however been better than that in most of our home yards. I offered him a deal. If I put more work into Gibraltar dockyard, could he deliver improvements in the cost and time for the completion of that work? He said he could. I subsequently fulfilled my side of the bargain and he delivered improvements on his.

At Devonport the T&GWU leader had a militant reputation. The management of the yard had tried every means of curbing his influence within the yard including advancing him from an industrial grade to a non-industrial grade. Even that didn't work. No doubt, when we first met, he thought that either the admiral would be a pushover or that whatever I said I couldn't deliver. But the issues were not for the Navy they were for the Government. I was very fortunate in finding a backdoor through which we could make contact outside the formality of a Whitley meeting. This opportunity came from a highly unusual source – the Britannia Beagles at the Royal Naval College at Dartmouth. My kennelman there was a dear old man of whom I was very fond, called John Memory. John Memory's son worked in the dockyard and was a good drinking friend of the dockyard T&GWU leader. I therefore used this connection to pass informal messages, which, although certainly not providing the answer to every question, were, in my mind, helpful in ameliorating a number of disputes and providing a very small additional degree of management good sense...

At the dockyard at Rosyth, the principal yard for refitting nuclear submarines, we were having considerable problems with the coppersmiths' union which was taking industrial action over take-home pay. Although their basic rate of pay as industrial workers was not high, the opportunities for voluntary overtime were great. I sat in at a meeting of the non-industrial Whitley committee at Rosyth under the chairmanship of the general manager of the yard. He was a man of small stature with an unusual personal style of management. He explained at some length that the industrial action being undertaken by the coppersmiths was totally unjustified by the level of their take-home pay when overtime was included. "Do you realise," he said to the assembled non-industrial leaders, "that the take-home pay of Mr 'Spitandcatchit', the leader of the coppersmiths' union, taken together with the take-home pay of his deputy was greater than my own?" "Do you realise," he went on, "that your general manager is only worth two coppersmiths?" There was a moment's shocked silence during which one of the non-industrial trade union leaders next to whom I was sitting leant over to me and said in a strong Scottish accent and a loud whisper, "Do you think, sir, that we should trade him in?"

During my time as CFS we attempted to set out in a draft White Paper, the way ahead for the dockyards. During a visit to the US navy yard in Norfolk, Virginia, I had been impressed by the much simplified overall structure of support management in which the dockyard management were directly responsible to the naval operational authorities who held the budget. The US Navy yard bid for naval work in competition with private yards. There was clearly scope for more efficient and effective ways of doing our own business which would involve in a much closer and more simply structured relationship between the Fleet Support Organisation, the Naval Staff, the naval procurement organisation under the Controller of the Navy and the fleet. Whilst I had the personal support from our own Navy Minister in this regard, the idea of the substantive change that was involved was more than the political and civil service bureaucracy could stand. Since then, there have been substantial changes that have been forced by continuing cuts in the defence budget. Whether these have also effectively addressed the dysfunctional problems of the Fleet Support Organisation, and the management style of the civilian workforce, is not clear to me. At the very least the problems will be of a different nature. Whether they produce an answer conducive to greater operational effectiveness and more acceptable to the fleet, I can only hope.

A major event during my time on the board was the 1977 Fleet Review at Spithead commemorating the Silver Jubilee of Her Majesty the Queen and attended by the Queen in her role as Lord High Admiral. The former Board of Admiralty shared with the sovereign the privilege of flying the special Board of Admiralty flag. This privilege was granted to the Navy Board when "proceeding as a board". For the review, we travelled together to Portsmouth thus proceeding as a board. Our wives came with us and my wife subsequently produced a rather splendid cartoon. It showed a small party of sailors carrying with some ceremony five large, thick planks over which was flying the Board Flag. It was entitled "The Board, travelling as a board".

The review, under the control of the Commander-in-Chief of Fleet, Admiral Sir Henry Leach, was an undoubted success. The dinner held in HMS ARK ROYAL at anchor at Spithead, at which the very large numbers who attended in the hangar were able to drink the Loyal Toast in the presence of Her Majesty, our Lord High Admiral, was an unforgettable experience, despite the appalling weather and some catering difficulties.

One of the innovations in the working of the Admiralty Board that were introduced by Terry Lewin, was that we should meet outside London from time to time. On one occasion when we were meeting in Portsmouth, as we broke for tea and strolled in the gardens of Admiralty House on a lovely summer's evening, Terry came up to me and said, "Jim, I want you to be the next Commander-in-Chief of the Fleet." This came as a total surprise and one of the best pieces of news that I had ever been fortunate to receive.

National and NATO Maritime Commanders-in-Chiefs 1968-1995
Back (L to R):
Sir Nick Hunt, Sir Julian Oswald, Sir Ben Bathurst, Sir Hugo White, Sir Bill O'Brian, Sir John Bush, Sir John Treacher, Sir Jim Eberle
Front (L to R):
Sir Wiliam Staveley, Sir Terry Lewin, Sir Edward Ashmore, Sir Henry Leach

Chapter 2

National and NATO Commander-in-Chief

"Human relationships are the essence of leadership and confidence, and are the vital threads running through all times at sea."
Admiral of the Fleet, Sir Edward Ashmore
"The Battle and the Breeze"

I arrived at Northwood, the shore headquarters of the Commander-in-Chief, Fleet CINCFLT on the morning of the 4th of May 1979. I was greeted by a guard of honour. As is normal practice, my take-over from Henry Leach was short. In addition to my national responsibilities as CINCFLT I also assumed the duties of NATO Commander-in-Chief, Channel, (CINCHAN); NATO Commander-in-Chief, Eastern Atlantic, (CINCEASTLANT); and Commander Task Force 345 (CTF345). The latter was a separate command function which was the operational authority for the ballistic missile force of Polaris fitted submarines. Within my headquarters was the Flag Officer Submarines, Admiral 'Tubby' Squires, the professional head of the submarine branch and responsible for all our submarines, both nuclear and conventional; and 18 Group, the RAF's maritime patrol aircraft, under the command of Air Marshal John Curtis. My national staff was under the charge of my Chief-of-Staff, Rear Admiral David Halifax – and a NATO staff under the charge of a highly competent Dutch rear admiral, Chris Krejger.

My remit was global in nature. East-West tensions were running high and apparently increasing. In the Middle East, Iran and Iraq were at war. In the Far East, the future of Hong Kong remained uncertain. In southeast Asia, political instabilities, particularly in Indonesia, posed potential threats to Britain's economic interests. In NATO as CHINCHAN, I was one of the three top military Commanders. In my national hat as CINCFLT, I was responsible for the operational efficiency of a range of capabilities from ballistic missile firing submarines, aircraft carriers, amphibious forces, anti-submarine forces down to small mine countermeasures and fishery protection craft. In Whitehall, it was becoming clear that political and inter-service battles over the defence budget lay not too far over the horizon.

My attention turned first to the fleet. I believed it was in good form despite the high intensity of the operational programme, which in some cases exceeded that of World War II, despite heavy fuel constraints caused by the shortage of funds. Such constraints were aggravated by dockyard refits that continued to over-run, and a shortage of equipment spare parts. There were also serious manning problems, the result of service pay having for many years lagged behind other sections of the community. The 1979 pay review had however been a significant boost to morale and I was keen to build on this.

My first signal to the fleet reflected a strong personal belief. It was to the effect that, despite such problems, I expected officers and men to have fun; and that I regarded fun as being an attitude of mind, rather than relating to a particular activity. I regarded fun as an essential ingredient of efficiency and not its enemy. Despite all the seagoing problems, my recent personal experience of our sea training organisation (FOST) and as Flag Officer Carriers and Amphibious Ships (FOCAS), had left me broadly content with the overall operational efficiency of our ships. I was also satisfied that the series of concentrated operational exercises (joint maritime courses) carried out in a simulated multi-threat environment in northern waters, usually under the command of one of the two flotilla flag officers, made a significant contribution to the fleet's effectiveness.

Nevertheless, I did not like the way that the frigate force was organised in its day-to-day business. The two seagoing flotilla flag officers, in whom I had great confidence, each commanded a force of several squadrons. Each squadron consisted of ships of the same class. This was an organisation that suited the 'technicos' and a period of peace – because each ship of the flotilla had the same equipment and could, in this technical

Admiral Eberle, NATO Commander-in-Chief, Ann Eberle & Queen Juliana of Netherlands

The Admiral gets operational

sense, readily exchange experiences and support each other within the squadron. In times of operational emergency and war, it would be necessary to form support groups for the protection of a carrier force, or amphibious force, or convoy. It was operationally essential for such support groups to have as wide a mix as possible of weapon and equipment capabilities. This would entail drawing individual ships from various squadrons. In my view it was necessary that the captains of these ships should have a considerable knowledge of the operational strengths and weaknesses of the other ships. Indeed I also took the view that the captains themselves should know each other well. If you were going to have to fight together, it was better that you should play at war together too. I therefore asked my staff to examine a possible restructuring of the squadron organisation to reflect an operational mix. In the event, I found that this was not practical because of the need to limit the number of technical experts in a squadron to cover the wide range of advanced equipments.

My next priority had to be towards NATO. The NATO military command arrangements were necessarily extensive and complex. In the very early days of the alliance two major NATO commanders were proposed. They were the Supreme Allied Commander, Europe (SACEUR) and the Supreme Allied Commander, Atlantic (SACLANT). The latter would have his headquarters in Norfolk, Virginia. Winston Churchill however would not accept putting the command of the British fleet under an American admiral on the far side of the Atlantic. Thus a third major NATO command was established, CINCHAN, who was to be a British admiral whose area of operations covered the approaches to the UK. Whilst both the areas of this command and the forces allocated to it were small compared with those of the other two major NATO commanders, CINCHAN was nevertheless given the status of one of the three major NATO commanders. Whether he was also a "Supreme Commander" was not addressed. This led to certain anomalies, where CINCHAN did not take part in some of the formal and informal NATO meetings attended by SACEUR and SACLANT. My predecessor addressed this anomaly. It was not a matter of personal status. The value of CINCHAN was that he represented the European nations in NATO in an otherwise American dominated forum. As a result of his efforts CINCHAN was accepted as a supreme commander and thus could represent a European military voice in such important committees as the NATO Nuclear Planning Group.

The balance of nuclear forces between NATO and the Warsaw Pact had been brought into question by the Russian deployment of a new nuclear missile, the SS20 which, while not of intercontinental range, did threaten the whole of western Europe. To redress this adverse balance, the US proposed to deploy a newly developed cruise missile with a nuclear warhead in western Europe. Such a deployment raised severe political problems in several of the NATO countries. I was concerned that this new situation represented a further escalation in the nuclear destructive power of both sides. From its earliest days the strategy of nuclear deterrence had been almost entirely developed in America. It involved a complex matrix of factors such that it became impossible to consider any reduction of the number of nuclear weapons by either side. If such a proposal were put forward, American strategists would argue that pulling out this one 'brick' would risk a collapse of the whole edifice of the nuclear strategy. I found this difficult to accept in the light of the fact that NATO had enough nuclear power to fire one nuclear weapon, the size of the Hiroshima bomb or greater, every few minutes throughout a period of four days. This would have been enough to destroy the world ten times over. It seemed to me that once was more than enough. Nuclear de-escalation should therefore be a policy option.

Furthermore, if cruise missiles were to be deployed, I suggested that many of the political difficulties with NATO governments could be overcome if they were deployed not on the ground but on submarines. However, my colleague, Admiral Harry Train, SACLANT, who was reflecting the very clear similar position held by the US Navy Department in Washington, vigorously opposed any such suggestion. There was clearly no way that I was going to get this proposal off the ground. On the 12th of December 1979, a

NATO Council meeting was held at foreign minister level to approve the deployment of nuclear cruise missiles on the ground in western Europe and in the UK as part of a twin track policy. The second track was the pursuit of an arms control strategy to reduce the number of Intermediate range nuclear missiles in Europe.

The Secretary General of NATO, Joseph Luns, formerly The Netherlands Foreign Minister for twelve years, chaired the meeting. As a chairman, he was by nature very relaxed. As CINCHAN, I was in attendance with my two colleagues, SACLANT and SACEUR. It was a very difficult meeting that lasted well into the night. Eventually unanimous agreement to deploy nuclear cruise missiles was obtained – though at several stages it seemed to me that the result of Joseph's natural good humour and ability to dismiss other arguments summarily was counter-productive. I admired Joseph Luns greatly but on this occasion I was forced to the conclusion that his 'hamming it up' brought the meeting near to failure on at least one occasion. The implementation of this decision continued to lead to NATO-wide political controversy; and in England to riots and demonstration at Greenham Common where the cruise missiles were to be deployed.

It was not only the deployment of the SS20s that was the cause of growing concern about the rising military strength of the Soviets. In early 1980, the US decided to release to the high political authorities in NATO a series of satellite photographs of the production of Soviet military equipment. These provided a chilling picture of their increasing capability to make war. The degree of detail revealed in these 'overheads' and the breadth of their coverage across the Soviet Union was most impressive to all. There were to be two presentations in The Hague. The first, led by General Bernie Rogers as SACEUR, dealt with Soviet tactical air and ground capability on the central front. The second dealt with the maritime situation, led by Harry Train, SACLANT and myself as CINCHAN. Overnight Harry Train and I received a very strong message from Joseph Luns saying that Bernie Rogers had "over done it" on the previous afternoon and had scared the living daylights out of his audience. Harry and I were being pressed to tone down what we had planned to say. The answer had to be "in no way". What we were showing was the real world in which we had to live; there was no value in pretending that things were better than they looked. Indeed they might even be worse.

A most welcome agreement had been reached by my predecessor that the Secretary General and the three major NATO commanders should meet informally three or four times a year to discuss the state of the alliance. Each of us in turn would choose the venue where business was mainly discussed over an excellent lunch. When we held our meeting at Northwood, I discovered that Joseph was an expert on the history of the Battle of Dogger Bank. The detailed issues of this defining naval engagement of World War I were usually associated with the alleged clash of personalities between the two admirals, Admiral Jellicoe and Admiral Beatty. Indeed, they are a continuing source of discussion. Looking at a painting of the battle hanging in my house, Joseph commented, "That painting represents the situation at 16:29 on the day of the battle when an order to turn to the north was given. I can tell that because of the direction of the wind at that time."

One question that I continued to ask was, "When and if hostilities between NATO and the Warsaw Pact broke out, who, what, where would be the political authority directing the war?" This was a question that Joseph continually refused to answer, on the grounds that to clarify this issue would disrupt the vital political cohesion of the alliance. My response was that it was better to consider the issue now than at a time when fighting between the two sides had erupted. Joseph responded by saying that when this happens it will be all up to you, the military commanders. I said, "No way. Politicians cannot abandon their responsibilities at such a stage." A 'staff answer' might have been that such a role would have fallen to NATO's Defence Council. In my view, the Council was totally unsuitable for making early policy decisions as would have been vital to the success of the military operations. Of course Washington, being the centre of control for NATO's nuclear power, would be the *de facto* centre of decision. There was, however, neither a formal nor informal organisation in the USA for NATO countries to represent their positions. Such a body had existed In NATO's formative years. It was known as the Standing Group - but it had long since ceased to exist. Fortunately the situation never arose when an answer to this question would have been vital.

However, I was well aware of a situation that did arise, when the NATO Planning Group were meeting in Germany, in the late autumn of 1980. Opposition to the Communist regime had been escalating throughout the year. In Moscow, the possibility of a successful Polish counter-revolution was being taken very seriously. East-West relations, following a series of seemingly unrelated incidents, were at a low ebb. During the meeting, we learned that satellite reconnaissance had revealed major Soviet forces in Poland leaving their barracks, apparently in full war fighting order. The situation did not look good. SACEUR requested approval to increase NATO's readiness on the central front by strengthening the military staff at a few of his forward operational headquarters. His request was refused.

NATO had a formal indicator system to help gauge a developing threat of war. There were some ten or more differing warning categories, each of which was colour coded from green to yellow to red, through a variety of tones. If SACEUR's request had been accepted, the situation with which we were presented would have caused one of the ten categories to move up one step. All the remainder stayed at green, i.e. normal. In the event, we received reports that the Russian forces were returning to their barracks. This incident did not increase my confidence in the likely validity or value of the warning system.

As a result of experience in exercises, my predecessor had briefed me that he had proposed a change in the SACEUR-CINCHAN command sea boundary in the approaches to the Baltic. This was where the command boundary ran through an area in which crucial operations were likely to take place if Soviet forces from the Baltic were to attempt to break out into the North Sea. The change of operational control from one area to the other involved ships in significant changes in operational procedures thereby inevitably reducing their fighting effectiveness. This proposal was strongly opposed by SACEUR, resulting in some friction at the highest level. I saw no purpose in continuing the argument, believing that it was more sensible to eliminate the procedural changes rather than change the boundaries. The latter would not solve the situation - it would only move its location. My staff was successful in achieving an agreement on procedures which effectively solved the problem.

Nevertheless, boundaries could present a problem as I discovered when I went on an operational visit to the NATO naval commander in north Norway. He was a Norwegian admiral whose chain of command ran through the NATO Commander-in-Chief (North) to SACEUR. The latter's naval boundary ran fifty miles to the north of North Cape. My boundary, as CINCEASTLANT adjoined his. I wanted to probe the sort of initiative that I could expect from him in times of high tension. I said to him,

"Let us assume that a high state of tension exists between NATO and the Warsaw Pact. We have seen a Russian amphibious force being mounted at Pechenga (part of the Russian northern fleet base structure). It has sailed and is now heading westward to pass some sixty miles to the north of North Cape. We know from signal intelligence that the destination of this force is Iceland and that it does not present a direct threat to Norway.

You have a force of well-equipped missile armed gunboats and small submarines. The weather is good and they would have no problem in reaching the Soviet force. However this force is in my area, not yours.

The formal procedure for getting you to take appropriate action would require me as CINCEASTLANT to signal to SACEUR requesting your support - which would then have to be passed up the line through CINCNORTH and COMNAVNORTH to you. It seemed unlikely that such a request would get through in time to be effective. Can I ask you what you would *do* in such a situation?"

I had hoped that his answer would be that he would put his forces to sea heading to intercept the Soviet force whilst informing his own chain of command, and CINCEASTLANT, that he had done so. He paused and looked hard at me and said, "I would feel very sorry for the Icelanders." I hoped that he had his tongue firmly in his cheek; but I was not very sure. I knew that the sentiment 'Norway for the Norwegians' was very strong.

I was taken to within a few hundred yards of the Norwegian-Russian border and somewhat beyond in a rather hairy helicopter trip. Fortunately there was a sensible arrangement of local interests between the Norwegians and the Soviets, which somewhat eased my concerns on East-West tensions, at least on NATO's northern flank.

Boundaries were also of concern to me in relation to France and particularly as the route of their ballistic missile firing submarines from Brest into the open oceans passed through NATO waters. In January 1980, I paid a visit to my opposite number in Brest, where I was able to visit a French nuclear submarine, whose apparent lack of machinery noise reduction techniques had surprised me. I was delighted also to visit the École Navale. There followed an offer of a visit to the French Mediterranean fleet based at Toulon where I was again warmly received at an outstanding dinner with the French Commander–in-Chief; although my naval assistant and I both succumbed to a nasty gastric attack that somewhat curtailed the following day's programme. These most welcome visits gave me a much better insight into the French naval capabilities. It was clear that the French were trying very hard to keep up with the advances in capability that NATO, led by the United States, had achieved. Nevertheless, they were lagging in many areas.

Much of my first six months in command was taken up by visits to the plethora of national and NATO authorities with whom my staff and I needed to deal. These included a formal call on the queen of The Netherlands, which I greatly enjoyed and appreciated. I had already formed a close relationship with the Commander-in-Chief of The Netherlands' navy and The Netherlands Defence

Minister. During this period SACEUR was General Al Haigh. I found him an impressive man; although I was somewhat concerned at his total dismissal of the value of the NATO Military Committee to which he owed formal allegiance. The Military Committee consisted of the chiefs-of-defence of each of the NATO nations who understandably met only infrequently. They were represented in Brussels by their 'MILREPS' who formed the military equivalent of the ambassadors to NATO who formed the 'PERMREPS'.

My first formal meeting with Al Haigh followed a NATO meeting at the NATO headquarters in Brussels. He had invited me down to his SHAPE headquarters at Mons. It was arranged that I would follow in my car directly behind the general. As was normal practice, we travelled at high speed accompanied by a police escort. After a very good lunch, I met appropriate senior members of his staff. It was a useful and friendly visit. After my departure, my naval assistant, Captain Colin Cooke-Priest told me that whilst we were having lunch, the aide had shown him the generals car. It had both armour and armament. In the boot was a machine gun that pointed directly backwards and could be operated from inside the car. I told Colin firmly that we were not again going to follow close behind the general's car.

When Al Haigh left NATO, he returned to America, where he underwent a heart bypass operation. Not long after, he was appointed as President Reagan's US Secretary of State. Much though I shared a great deal of the considerable admiration that he had gained in both political and military circles in Europe, it seemed to me that his lack of depth of knowledge and experience in the American domestic political system might not rest easily with the US foreign policy task. In the event, I did think that Al Haigh as US Secretary of State appeared a very different person to the Al Haigh that I had known. Indeed, his performance in the State Department was widely criticised throughout America. His manoeuvrings with regard to Argentina in the run-up to the South Atlantic war were not all well received in London. Only the unstinting support of the UK by Casper Weinberger and the US

Department of Defence prevented what might have been the cause of a significant downturn in the UK-US relationship. Later however I understood from a distinguished heart surgeon that such personality changes are not unusual following heart operations which clearly affect the circulation of blood to the brain. His successor as SACEUR was General Bernie Rogers. He was of a very different character to Al Haigh, being far more aware of NATO's political sensibilities and with a much calmer manner.

NATO ran a number of large-scale exercises, some which were played only on paper and others that involved the large scale deployment of ships at sea. These exercises sometimes ended with a preliminary nuclear phase. In a previous such exercise, SACLANT made the appropriate procedural precautionary preparations for the possible use of tactical nuclear weapons, as was called for in the exercise play. He was strongly criticised for what he did. When we reached a similar situation in a subsequent exercise, Harry Train told me that he was going to refuse to participate in this part of the exercise as a result of the personal criticism made of him previously. I decided that to make exercise play, I would participate in my role as CINCHAN and CINCEASTLANT. I sought through the proper command channels and procedures a conditional release of several nuclear depth charges on account of the submarine threat posed to the NATO strike fleet operating in my area. The first reaction to this was from Bernie Rogers who phoned me to ask that I should withdraw my request on the grounds that it represented a threat to SACEUR's request, which was for conditional release of a considerable number of nuclear weapons on the central front. These were required in order to contain a breakthrough by Soviet ground forces. He feared that the NATO political authorities, realising that we were in danger of approaching escalation to a strategic nuclear exchange, would choose my request rather than his own because it was less escalatory. I was not prepared to withdraw, not least because of the need to exercise both the military and political play in this very difficult and contentious area.

I also received word that Margaret Thatcher was seriously angry on the grounds of 'what was this British commander doing, asking for preliminary authority for the release of nuclear weapons under certain conditions without first asking her'. Although realising that this represented a strong 'handbag' challenge to me, I was reinforced in my view that I had done the right thing. It brought into focus the concern that I had so often expressed to the Secretary General about who was the political authority running the war. These were not British nuclear weapons. They were NATO weapons and belonged to the United States and not to Britain. Even the Polaris missiles in the UK ballistic firing submarines were declared to NATO; although the submarines themselves remained under UK national command and control - hence my own role as CTF 345. I found this small episode a little surprising since, on an earlier occasion I had chanced to meet the Prime Minister in the VIP lounge at the airport at Northolt. She was returning from Italy with Lord Carrington and stopped me to ask about a nuclear deterrence paper that was coming before the Cabinet the next day. I had been impressed by her grasp of the issues.

One of the fundamental missions of SACLANT was to position the US strike fleet carriers in the north Norwegian Sea to present a threat to the Soviet northern fleet and its bases. I regarded this as an operation that involved enormous risks from the counterforce of Russian long-range aircraft and submarines in their 'backyard'. However, I well remembered a private session with Admiral Ike Kidd who was SACLANT at his NATO headquarters at Norfolk, VA. I had then been FOCAS (COMCARGRUTWO). He was a man of immense experience, greatly respected and liked by all. Our conversation had started on the subject of the political control of war. To my surprise he had seen and read the paper that I had produced as a result of my defence scholarship at Oxford. To my even greater surprise he told me that he thought it one of the best papers relative to command in NATO that he had seen. Our conversation turned to some of the NATO war-gaming exercises that we had carried out at the US Naval War College at Newport, Rhode Island. I expressed some concern as to whether even the self-defence capabilities of the strike fleet would permit it to operate successfully for very long in this north Norwegian Sea area. I can vividly remember Ike standing before a wall map and jabbing his stubby finger at the north Norwegian Sea saying, "Jim, we've got to get them up there. We've got to get them up there."

In the first of my two large-scale quadrennial NATO live exercises, the US strike fleet was under the command of Admiral Stan Turner. He fooled everybody by operating his carriers in total radio silence so that no one either on the blue side or the red side knew where he was. It was an interesting move that rather ruined much of the exercise – but I was not sure how realistic that would have been in real war. I had previously come across Stan Turner in strategic discussions at the War College where we were both inclined to be critical of some areas of NATO policy. We became particularly good friends. Stan's next appointment was as the NATO commander in the southern NATO region, CINCSOUTH, whose headquarters were in Naples. Later, under President Jimmy Carter, he became head of the US Central Intelligence Agency. During a visit to Washington, I was able to assist the British Intelligence authorities by speaking to him on a personal and informal basis to help resolve certain difficulties arising from unilateral US action. The problem was that the US were denying the UK certain basic intelligence information in contravention of a long standing formal agreement on the mutual sharing of intelligence information.

Whilst NATO business occupied a great deal of my time, I was able to keep close watch on the day-to-day business of the UK fleet from my daily operational and intelligence briefings which took place at the start of play each day in the "hole"– the underground headquarters which housed both the NATO staff and the UK fleet operational staff. The threat from Iran and Iraq to international shipping in the Persian Gulf was of constant concern and necessitated our keeping two frigates or destroyers constantly on station there – the Armilla patrol. In view of the mining threat, we also deployed a mine countermeasure squadron from the UK. The West Indies guard ship, whose tasks included anti drug smuggling operations, was another continuing commitment – although service there was a good deal more popular amongst ships' companies than that in the Gulf. We also continued to plan and execute an occasional 'round the world' deployment, wherever possible centred on an aircraft carrier in support of Britain's overseas interests and as an earnest of British commitment to global security.

Occasional unforeseeable incidents kept the operational staff fully on their toes. Shortly before Christmas 1979, the deployment of the Soviet aircraft carrier KIEV from the Kola peninsular, the Soviet northern fleet base, accompanied by three escorts and a tanker, caused a flurry of excitement. She passed north of the Faroe Islands into the Atlantic, before turning south and in due course entering the Mediterranean. On the way, she was shadowed by Norwegian, Danish, British, French and Portuguese war ships and maritime patrol aircraft. The co-ordination of this operation was undertaken by my CINCEASTLANT staff in the 'hole'. The unexplained and continuing operations of a Soviet research vessel in a very small area in the eastern Atlantic gave rise to much unresolved speculation. A defect discovered during the periodic docking of a British SSBN. This required the unscheduled and careful replacement of the on-patrol Polaris submarine, an operation which required very sensitive handling in order that it could be achieved without any break in the secure UK deterrent posture. The unexpected appearance of a Soviet nuclear submarine in a new area of operations was often the cause of a lengthy discussion at my morning briefing. The occasional shadowing operations carried out both by NATO and Soviet submarines; and urgent operational defects in our own deployed surface ships ensured that life in the hole was seldom dull.

However, not all OPDEFs (Operational Defect Reports) in the fleet were matters of equipment failures. Whilst the Commander-in-Chief was embarked in the HMS SHETLAND on a visit to the islands, the following exchange between the ship and fleet headquarters at Northwood is recorded:

From HMS SHETLAND to Northwood
For Flag Lieutenant from Commander-in-Chief
OPDEF 1/79. Lower half upper port side gnasher disintegrated when tackling particularly succulent scatata sweet.
No pain, but intake limited to 85% normal due irritating discomfort. Would appreciate toothwright assistance if practicable on return Northwood.

From CINCFLT (Rear Link) to CINCFLT (Flag) in HMS SHETLAND
Big Jim afloat in waters polar
Crunched his lunch and lost a molar
Put about and sail me south
Send an opdef 'bout me mouth'.
The Fleet's toothwright's in a stew
To find new teeth for Jim to chew:
Don't worry Doc, and don't take fright-
Our Jim's bark is worse than his bite!
He'll sail the sea for brand new ventures
In collar stars[2] and dazzling dentures

The very considerable administrative task of the UK surface fleet I was able to leave in the extremely capable hands of my national Chief-of-Staff, Rear Admiral David Halifax. He was later relieved by Rear Admiral William Stavely who in due course was himself appointed as CINCFLT. He was a highly efficient officer, but one of a very different character from myself. When I was rung up by the First Sea Lord to ask my agreement that he should be appointed as my Chief-of-Staff, I accepted with words to the effect that, due to our differing temperaments, this appointment would either be somewhat difficult or a great success - and that I would do my very best to make it the latter. I was delighted that our mutual efforts for success were well fulfilled. Sadly, he died at an early age, not long after retiring as the First Sea Lord.

In Whitehall the battle for cuts in the defence budget was beginning to hot up. When John Nott had taken over as Secretary

---

[2] *I always refused to wear shoulder boards to indicate rank. I wore silver stars on my collar in lieu.*

of State for Defence in 1981, he had been briefed by his civil service advisers that the level of the defence budget was unsustainable. Significant cuts in the defence programme would have to be made. He therefore asked the three chiefs-of-defence to tell him what were the non-essential items in their budgets. Fearing that anything they offered would inevitably be cut; they replied that there was effectively nothing in their budgets that was non-essential. John Nott was therefore left with little alternative than to make up his own mind on where the axe should fall; as expressed in broad terms in the famous 'Bermuda telegram'. His planned cuts were based on questionable assumptions, and fell principally on the Navy. The subsequent position of the Navy was not helped by a growing personal antipathy between the Defence Minister and the First Sea Lord; and by the failure of the three service chiefs to work together, despite the formal structure of the Chiefs-of-Staff Committee.

These matters were not my direct concern; but nevertheless it was right that the commander-in-chief should express any concerns that he had on the future size and shape of the fleet[3]. My particular concern was in regard to the future frigate programme in which a new class of frigate, the Type 23, was set to replace many of the existing frigate force consisting of some sixty ships. The Type 23 design was large, highly capable and very expensive. In my view it was difficult to classify it in the frigate category. It was more the equivalent of our pre and post World War II cruisers. Even at the height of the British Empire we could never have afforded a force of cruisers of the size that we had set as a target for the frigate force. The argument evolved into the old age dilemma of quality versus quantity. It was clear to me that the First Sea Lord did not share this view. Although the Controller of the Navy, Admiral John Fieldhouse, who was responsible for the ship programme, also did not support my position, he clearly understood it... He expressed his view perfectly in saying, "Jim, in any quantity-quality argument, quantity must always win – provided you have enough of it."

---

[3] *The Commander-in Chief Fleet is now a member of the Navy Board.*

Unfortunately the quantity-quality argument became confused by another 'chestnut' that became known as 'the short, fat ship' versus 'the long, thin ship'. This arose out of some tank model testing, which indicated that a certain hull shape did not comply with the deeply traditional view that the speed, for any given propulsive power, depended on the 'l/d' ratio - that is to say that the speed of any hull through the water is dependent on the ratio of the hull length to its breadth. If the tank testing results were to be correct in the full scale, then it gave rise to all sorts of other hull design possibilities, including a modular construction, with considerable advantages in terms of weapon system fitting. This could result in a ship that was more flexible in design and a good deal cheaper to build and maintain. As happens from time to time, this debate created more heat than light. Although as far as I am aware the advantageous tank testing results were never disproved – they were just disbelieved. 'The establishment' rallied round to throw out this outrageous challenge to conventional thought. It was a pity that this confused the arguments about the cost of frigates – one that was soon to be highlighted by the 1992 defence review which reduced our frigate force from some sixty ships to forty-two. Today it numbers in the twenties. The basic quantity-quality argument is, I fear, still not dead.

It was also at about this time that I learned that I was to be relieved in the spring of 1981. I understood that my next appointment would be as Commander-in-Chief of the Naval Home Command. I was not best pleased. I was thoroughly enjoying my job and was concerned that my departure might undermine the success that my predecessor had achieved in the recognition of the post of the NATO Commander-in-Chief, Channel as fully equivalent to that of the two other supreme commanders. The tour of duty of the latter was normally four years. I further argued that this rapid turnover was expensive and detrimental to NATO military solidarity and political effectiveness. It had taken me the best part of a year to do my rounds of national and NATO authorities – and it would now not be long before I would need to start my round of farewells. To me, this was highly unsatisfactory on almost every count. However, I had done my research and established that I was not being short-changed in that my tenure of almost two years stood in the middle of the period of tenure of my recent predecessors.

I thus took an informal opportunity at one of the NATO Defence Committee meetings to present my views to our Secretary of State for Defence, Francis Pym – who said he understood this and agreed with me. The scene shifts to a subsequent NATO Nuclear Planning Group meeting in Norway. It was a beautiful, clear autumn morning. With a little time to spare before the meeting, our Chief-of-Defence, Admiral Terry Lewin, and I took a quiet stroll round the harbour. I waxed strongly on my view. Warming to my theme, I finished by saying, "And what is more, when I expressed these views informally to Francis Pym the other day, he said that he agreed with me. I dispute the view that it would be difficult to do. All that would be required would be for the Secretary-of-State to say to you that all future appointments at this level should average between three and five years – pray make it so. Indeed having discussed it with him I don't see why the hell he doesn't do so." In his marvellously tactful and expressive way Terry replied, "Jim, the reason he doesn't do so is because I have advised him not to." My respect for Terry allowed me no other course than to say, "OK, boss." I continued to make the arrangements for my farewell calls on the appropriate international military and political authorities; one of whom said to me, "But Jim, you've only just arrived." I managed to hold my tongue.

Whilst visiting the State of Georgia, USA, in November 1980, I had the opportunity to make an informal call on the Governor, George D. Busbee. I was delighted, and a little surprised, to be awarded by him a commission as Admiral in the Georgian Navy. I did not know that Georgia had ever had a navy. However, at that time, neither he nor I could have been aware that, two hundred and forty-five years before, John Wesley, a relative of the English branch of my family and founder of the Methodist Church, together with Bishop Nitchsman, a senior member of the

Moravian Church with which my German family were very closely connected, had crossed the Atlantic from Britain together. In the same ship was General Oglethorpe, the British appointed First Governor of Georgia, then a new British colony. I now wear my title as Admiral of the Georgian Navy with pride.

Reflecting my national worldwide responsibilities, I visited Australia, New Zealand, Hong Kong and Delhi. I also had a schedule call at Bombay where, at the naval dockyard, I saw small Russian designed ships that seemed to be much more heavily armed than their western counterparts. The RAF had provided a VC10 aircraft, which was also involved in other work in this region, to carry me. I find flying as a passenger somewhat boring. I therefore asked for the privilege of being able to sit in the jump seat behind and between the two pilots when we were carrying out the interesting bits, take-off and landing. We were coming in to Bombay in vile monsoon weather conditions. Some time before the passenger terminal at Bombay airport had been burnt down. This was important to the passengers but more so to the aircrew since the control tower had been built on top of the passenger terminal. The landing aids had thus been reduced to a very basic talk down system.

As we began our approach I was aware that the pilot was not happy with his directions. As we approached an altitude of a thousand feet, which was the limit below which we were not permitted to go without the pilot having a clear sight of the runway and its approach lights, a confusing pattern of lights flashed up. The pilot clearly did not recognise them and called for an overshoot. The engineer brought up the landing gear. The second pilot opened the throttles and the aircraft climbed away with the pilot calling on the radio "overshoot, overshoot, overshoot". There was a short pause and I heard the temporary tower reply, "Roger your overshoot. What is your problem?" I was no little concerned when I heard the pilot respond, "The runway that you just lined me up on was several hundred feet long and eighteen thousand feet wide". The ground controller apologised. "I am very sorry", he said, "I do hope it's not going to be another day like yesterday." I was very happy when we eventually got down safely.

In the late summer of 1980 I was informed by Whitehall that the new Governor of the Falkland Islands, Sir Rex Hunt, would be coming to call on me. Regrettably I was very ignorant of my exact responsibilities with regard to the security of the Islands. I was aware that I had administrative responsibility for the small force of Royal Marines that were garrisoned there – but was far from clear where operational responsibility for their security rested. The staff answer did not encourage me. It was that full operational responsibility for the security of the Islands rested in Whitehall with the Ministry of Defence. My concern was that, in my view, the MoD structure was entirely unsuited to the operational command of anything – and as far as I was aware there were no realistic plans for the defence of the Islands.

My meeting with Sir Rex centred on the planned withdrawal by the Navy Department of HMS ENDURANCE, the South Atlantic guard ship. This was on the grounds that, in the light of the government cuts in the defence budget, the Navy no longer had sufficient funds to justify this deployment. As a result of this meeting, I told my staff that I was very unhappy with the situation, which I did not understand, and told them to arrange for me to visit the Islands. Their short reply was, "Boss, you don't have the time." This aggravated me since I suffered from the weakness that if somebody told me I couldn't do something, my response was to say, "In that case, tell me how I can." My staff were as usual correct. I thought that the best I could do was to lobby against the Navy Department's proposal to withdraw ENDURANCE. I got little change from the First Sea Lord who argued that the ship's role was now entirely political and if the Foreign Office wanted to keep the ship there, they could pay for it.

I further took up the matter direct and personally with the Foreign Secretary, Lord Carrington. He agreed that the Foreign Office thought it unwise to withdraw the ship – and had written to the Ministry of Defence to say so. From the MoD's response, it was clear that the view of the First Sea Lord held sway. This, said

Peter Carrington, was ridiculous because the FCO did not have that sort of money in its budget. However, the future of the Falkland Islands was not on the government's agenda. Despite a short scare at the end of the year about Argentine intentions, which required me to prepare a small deterrent task-force to send to the South Atlantic, nothing was done. Shortly afterwards, this force was stood down. By then, I had shot off all my available ammunition - and the security situation within the NATO area was heating up.

I do not suggest that had it been possible for me to visit the Islands that the outcome of the political dispute with Argentina would have been any different. Subsequently, however, I found out that my view about the Navy Department's suitability for operational command was not too far wide of the mark. The Captain of ENDURANCE, Nick Barker, had for some time been aware that the ship's relationship with the Argentine navy, which had always been co-operative and friendly, was subtly changing. His concerns by signal addressed to the Admiralty were ignored on the grounds that Nick Barker was merely wanting to continue his South Atlantic command, which he was rightly much enjoying. His concerns were also being expressed informally to the embassy staff in Buenos Aires. However, an unfortunate personal tension had arisen between the embassy and Captain Barker over a domestic matter concerning the ambassador. The embassy thus distrusted the reports being delivered from ENDURANCE and did not relay these concerns to the FCO. The rest is history.

My time at Northwood was a particularly happy one. My programme was always very full but the variety of national and NATO elements allowed me to keep in personal touch with the many senior and junior members of my large staff. Indeed the occasional staff cocktail party held from time to time in the large garden of my house was always a particularly happy occasion. Furthermore I had the facilities to give good dinner parties in the house for visiting senior 'firemen' from home and abroad. Although Northwood is very much a populated and popular suburb of London, there was still the occasional patch that was not built over. One of these adjoined the end of my garden. The house itself was at night illuminated by security floodlights. With my ear well tuned to the countryside it was not long before I recognised the barking of foxes. On several occasions I had looked out of my bedroom window to see a fox in the floodlights. In Devon, I had always been somewhat fascinated by those who could, by imitating the bark of a fox, call a fox close to them; usually so that it could be shot – for foxes were a considerable threat, not only to poultry, but also to new born lambs. I decided that my new environment was an opportunity for me to try and practice the art of fox calling which I had attempted without much success in Devon.

One early morning in the summer I slipped on an old pair of slacks and jersey and went down to the far end of my garden, where there was a tennis court. The secret of fox calling is to 'squeak', a noise that is the alarm call of a rabbit. I stood quietly in the middle of the tennis court and started to squeak, a noise which one can generate with the use of one's lips and the back of one's hand. I squeaked for some time with no success. It then occurred to me that in this urbanised area, the foxes were more accustomed to emptying dustbins than catching rabbits. But I didn't know how to imitate a dustbin. So I began to bark like a fox. Nothing happened so I returned to an attempt to squeak like a rabbit. After a short while I heard a rustling in the long grass at the bottom of the tennis court. I stood very still, and before many moments a beautiful young fox appeared moving along the side netting of the tennis court. It stopped and looked in my direction. After a few moments it turned tail and disappeared. I now did not know whether it was my barking or my squeaking that had attracted the fox.

My mission accomplished, I was delighted and walked slowly back towards the house. As I progressed up the path, I continued making barking noises so as to keep up the pretence. Unfortunately, my chief steward had just woken up and was looking out of his bedroom window at the top of the house to a beautiful morning. To his considerable surprise he saw the commander-in-chief dressed in an old sweater and slacks "walking up the path from the tennis court making the most extraordinary noises." Thereafter, whenever the house staff felt that the admiral might be feeling a need for some relaxation and could not be found in the house, they would say that he had probably gone down to the bottom of the garden to talk to the foxes.

The situation got worse. Late one fine summer evening, I was again at the bottom of the garden and heard a fox barking nearby. I managed to locate the fox which I saw sitting on the far side of an adjacent field. I took the opportunity to practice by responding to the foxes bark with my own imitation. To my delight this went on for some minutes. As the evening light started to fade, I saw the fox make a movement and disappear into the gloom. From the gate before which it had been sitting, emerged a human figure. It turned out to be the local farmer. He called out in my direction, "I've lost one of my cows. What are you doing - have you seen it by any chance?" At this moment my wits failed me and I replied, "I'm very sorry, I haven't. It is only the admiral barking at the foxes."

The local residents were, I knew, remarkably ignorant about what went on in this large naval establishment in their area – but they thought it had something to do with the Navy and a British and NATO admiral who was responsible for the defence of the country from the Russian navy. I am not sure quite what effect it had when they learned in the local pub that he spent his spare time talking to foxes.

Chapter 3

Commander-in-Chief, Naval Home Command

> *"May the great God whom I worship grant to my country and for the benefit of Europe in general a great and glorious victory, and may no misconduct of anyone tarnish it, and may humanity after victory be the predominant feature in the British Fleet."*
> Admiral Lord Nelson before the Battle of Trafalgar, 1805

I turned over my command as Commander-in-Chief of the Fleet to Admiral Sir John Fieldhouse, a submariner, in full confidence that the surface ships as well as the submarines would be in very good hands. I realised that my own new appointment as Commander-in-Chief, Naval Home Command was placing me in a holding pattern, possibly prior to retirement. My predecessor as CINCNAVHOME was Admiral Sir Dick Clayton, a former Naval Board colleague whom I held in very high regard. He was himself retiring from the Navy. Whatever my own future might hold I was as usual determined to enjoy myself. One of the great pleasures of the Home Command was that I flew my flag in HMS VICTORY, a ship in commission in the Royal Navy, having its own serving captain and ship's company.

VICTORY is also a national monument, open to the general public for whom the ship's company serve as ship keepers and act as guides. Nevertheless, I was able to use Nelson's great cabin for formal naval dinner parties, a privilege which I used regularly. People were willing to cross many oceans to dine aboard VICTORY. It was an occasion that was deeply memorable for all the Navy's guests. It was the proper place to mark the raising of the MARY ROSE from the Solent, a dinner being hosted by HRH The Prince of Wales and Princess Diana, for whom my son had acted as ADC. The entry of the 12-metre yacht 'Victory' in the America's Cup was also good cause for a ship-borne celebration. From time to time, I also used Captain Hardy's cabin for my work when I found my normal shore-side office too distracting; I was also able to use the lower gun deck for the wedding reception of my daughter Sarah, who was married in the dockyard church.

My turnover with Dick Clayton was appropriately brief. Apart from the challenge of reducing the training load in the Home Command following the previous year's defence review under the programme title 'Slimtrain', I did not see too many current challenges in my new command. I had a substantial headquarters staff that were, at least on paper, responsible for the execution of naval training policy, the Second Sea Lord being responsible for its formation. However, its execution was effectively in the hands of the highly professional staff of the shore training establishments whose location was principally in the Portsmouth area.

I therefore set about a programme of visits to establishments in the Home Command. I also brought one of my horses from Devon so that I could enjoy some fox hunting. I also took time to provide personal support for the Portsmouth command's Motor Cycle Club as its president. I had always disliked motorcycles, not least having fallen off whilst learning to ride one during my sub-lieutenants' flying course. Falling off a horse was one thing with which I was familiar – falling off a motorbike was something else. I also regarded them as a menace on the roads. However, my predecessor was a very keen and active motor-cyclist – I was never sure that he had a car, other than his official one. However, during our short turnover I had responded to his strong plea that I should take on this not very onerous duty. The members, he said, were a very good lot. Indeed they were. My aversion to motor-cycling was almost overcome – but not to the extent where I was honour bound to accept a ride on the pillion of a super-bike. I regarded pillion-riding as involving a very inelegant posture in relation to the driver - and positively dangerous. However minor and unimportant such very minor administrative tasks might seem, I never doubted that a direct short circuit from the top of the tree to its roots was an important element in leadership. For me, participation in sporting activities was an ideal way of achieving this.

Although my direct responsibilities were now in the support field, I could not tear myself away from the serious operational implications of the cuts that were being imposed on the Navy by the recent Defence Review. In May 1991, I wrote a personal letter to Paul Nitze, a greatly respected former Secretary of the US Navy, whom I had got to know well, asking him to talk with the US Secretary, Casper Weinberger, and US Navy Secretary John Lehman, both of whom I knew in my former NATO role, to make sure that they were thoroughly aware of the implications of John Nott's Defence Review. I feared that the UK government's decisions could lead to a shift of UK defence policy from conventional towards nuclear forces. This would have involved a return to a 'trip-wire' strategy. Furthermore we were not facing up to the unprecedented build up of Soviet conventional forces; and the UK reductions might encourage other European countries also to reduce their conventional contributions to NATO.

However, the events of the Falklands War in the following year caused some of the Naval Defence Review reductions to be put into reverse, particularly the phasing out of the aircraft carriers.

In early 1982, disturbing reports of Argentine naval operations in the South Atlantic began to arouse some of the concerns that I had about the South Atlantic in my last appointment as CINCFLT. On the 1st of April, after preliminary moves in the South Georgia region, the Argentine forces landed on the Falkland Islands. Initially there had been differing political views in Westminster as to how we should react to the Argentine moves. However, the First Sea Lord, in the absence of the Chief-of-Defence who was abroad on an official visit, went down to the House of Commons on the Wednesday afternoon and persuaded the Prime Minister that a naval taskforce could be mounted that would be able to recover the islands. On the Thursday, we received a signal from the Admiralty to prepare a taskforce for operations in the South Atlantic to sail as soon as possible. We were fortunate in that it was nearly Easter and that many of the ships of the fleet were already in their base ports or were due there very shortly. A taskforce was therefore ordered to sail on the following Monday.

The preparations were intense. On the Sunday afternoon I walked round the dockyard at Portsmouth talking to officers and sailors wherever I could. I visited HMS HERMES, where the captain was involved in detailed intelligence briefings. On leaving the ship, I stood at the bottom of one of the gangways watching stores being loaded by dockyard workers. One of them turned to me and said:

"How are they on board, sir?"
I replied, "They're fine, but a little bit apprehensive at the possibility of their going to war."
"But if they go to war, some of them may not come back."
"That's right – that is what happens in war."
"But they're so young, Sir." (Indeed, the average age of those in HERMES was probably about twenty-one).

On the Monday morning the taskforce sailed, witnessed by a large, cheering crowd of families and local population. This splendidly rapid reaction was typical of what young officers had always been taught. In manoeuvres at sea when an escorting ship was ordered to change its station, the first reaction of the officer-of-the-watch was to ring down for maximum speed and start going in the right direction. He then worked out exactly where he was supposed to go and adjusted his course and speed accordingly. It was a modification of the old adage that was applied to some car drivers (all of them in Italy) who manoeuvred their vehicles on the road according to the sequence 'act–signal–think'.

In the case of the Falkland Islands, there was little time to consider what action they could expect to take when they got there. The taskforce therefore headed for Ascension Island which became the final launching pad for the operation. The development of the detailed plans for the recovery of the Islands took some weeks, during which much rearrangement amongst the fleet was required. The very rapid response of a major element of the force in sailing from Portsmouth undoubtedly sent a strong political signal. However there was little doubt in my mind that, had we thought a bit more carefully about exactly what we were going to do when we reached the South Atlantic, we would have arrived at the Islands earlier than we did. Time was also of the essence – as the South Atlantic winter was closing in.

During this period, a strong rumour began circulating in the dockyard that VICTORY was being prepared for operations in the South Atlantic as flagship. After some investigation, I discovered the origin of this 'happy thought'. Some time before, it had been found that the number of the smaller iron cannon balls displayed in the ship had been reducing – probably due to visitors taking them as souvenirs. It was therefore decided to replace them with wooden look-a-likes. However, even these were found to 'walk'. In February, the captain of VICTORY had placed a requisition on the dockyard for a number of new ones to replace those that had been stolen. As luck would have it, this requisition came to the top of the dockyard's priority list just after the taskforce had sailed.

It was several weeks after the surrender of the Islands to the Argentines that the taskforce arrived in the Southern Ocean. Shortly after that, on a Sunday evening, the doorbell of Admiralty House rang. I went to the front door to find my Chief-of-Staff, Rear Admiral Trevor Spraggs, an excellent officer of the Instructor branch. He said to me, "HMS SHEFFIELD has been sunk." I immediately asked him about casualties and learned that there had been a number killed. It was that event that confirmed to the whole navy and the country that we had a war on our hands.

As CINCNAVHOME I had the responsibility for dealing with all the aspects of family support for those in the taskforce and for the reporting of casualties. A centre for handling these matters had been set up in the naval barracks at Portsmouth together with appropriate procedures and communications. The organisation swung swiftly into operation and worked well. There were of course some errors and mistakes particularly where men of the same name were serving in ships which had taken damage and casualties. My own son was serving in HMS ARGONAUT that was hit by two bombs, neither of which exploded. Had they done so the ship would undoubtedly have been lost and my son would have been killed. I told my wife only that my son's ship had been damaged - but that our son, as far as I was aware, had not been a casualty.

In the very early phase of the operational planning I had had some personal doubts about the command structure for this operation. Full operational command was to be held by the Commander-in-Chief, Fleet at Northwood. In the forward area the command of naval forces was to be divided between the two aircraft carriers HMS HERMES and INVINCIBLE and their supporting escorts and the landing forces operating inshore. In the event, this did cause some difficulties of priority in the use of the carrier borne aircraft for the defence of the offshore taskforce and the inshore landing forces. Nevertheless the availability of satellite communications between Northwood and the forward area commanders was vital to our success. At home, there was very close co-operation between my successor, John Fieldhouse, Terry Lewin, the Chief of Defence Staff, and the Prime Minister.

In the area of operations such close co-operation was difficult to achieve, mainly due to communication difficulties. This was the cause of some serious tension with London. When the first landings at San Carlos had been successfully completed, further time was needed to consolidate the bridgehead. This was understood in Whitehall. Mrs Thatcher, however, became very concerned about the delay in moving out from the bridgehead to engage the main Argentine forces. Messages were despatched from Whitehall to the effect that if a move out had not been initiated within twenty-four hours, the ground force commander at the bridgehead, Brigadier Julian Thompson, would be relieved of his command. This delay had also been fuelled by an almost unbelievable misunderstanding of the role of 3 Brigade, which had established the bridgehead; and that of 5 Brigade, which was embarked in the merchant ship, QUEEN ELIZABETH. It was thought that it would be 5 Brigade's task to conduct the breakout and to lead subsequent operations.

In the event, the Paras of 3 Brigade, under the command of Lieutenant Colonel H. Jones, moved out from San Carlos in time and undertook the successful assault on Argentine forces at Goose Green, although the colonel himself was killed. He was posthumously awarded a VC for his part in this epic action. This operation was in full concert with the fundamental concept of the battle from General Jeremy Moore, who was the overall ground force commander, that an initial move to inflict a very early defeat against an element of the Argentine force was his first priority, so establishing in the minds of the Argentines the idea of the total superiority of the British force.

It was at this time that we held one of our regular but infrequent Commander-in-Chief Home Committee meetings which were arranged to take place at an RAF air station. In the earlier phases of the operation in South Georgia one of the Argentine prisoners who had been taken was a marine lieutenant by the name of Estes who had long been accused of atrocities during Argentina's long internal war. He had in particular been charged with the murder of a Swedish nurse. There was no doubt that Estes was a nasty piece of work. He was being returned for custody in the United Kingdom. As CINCNAVHOME I had received a request from Whitehall to make arrangements for his custody on arrival. We were not quite sure how best to set about this since we could not find a precedent. We initially asked the gunnery school at Whale Island to prepare appropriate accommodation. However, my staff then discovered that under Queen's Regulations the custody of prisoners was a task for the army. I accordingly passed on the task to my army counterpart, General John Stannier.

Understandably, the crisis about the breakout was very much a matter of private conversation between John Stannier and me. One lunch, as we sat on either side of the Station Commander, I leaned over to John to apologise for having 'sloping shoulders', referring to my action in passing responsibility to him for the custody of Estes. The noise level was high and John had some difficulty in understanding what I was talking about. I repeated more loudly "Estes". John still did not get the message. After further explanation he responded that he didn't know what the hell I was talking about. It transpired that he thought it was about sanitary towels. From that moment Estes was code named Tampax, a codename that was continued throughout his incarceration in the UK.

When the operation had been terminated by the surrender of the Argentine forces in the Falkland Islands, the ships of the naval taskforce returned to Portsmouth for a tremendous welcome led by the Queen and Prince Philip. That evening I invited the commanding officers of twenty of these ships (see p.49) all of whom had served with me in my last appointment as CINCFLT, to dine with me in VICTORY in Nelson's great cabin. It was a most moving occasion with resonance of Nelson's 'Band of Brothers'. The commanding officers had not met face to face since before the beginning of the war. The conversation was dominated by sharing experiences. "Do you remember that night when you suddenly dashed off up to the north? I never understood what the hell you were up to." Then the reply, "I had just received an intercept which I thought came from an Argentine submarine. I didn't tell you immediately in case our tactical net was being intercepted. It was actually a false alarm." I felt a sense of personal pride in the performance of all the commanding officers.

I also felt pride in the spirit of their ships' companies which had been superb despite casualties amongst ships and people. When HMS COVENTRY was attacked by aircraft late in the war and had had to be abandoned, a young electrical officer told me that his life raft was a few hundred yards away from the ship when the ship capsized. As they sorted themselves out, the officer heard a plaintive voice from one of his young sailors lying on the floor of the life raft, "Sir?" "Yes." "Sir, does this mean that there will no longer be rounds tonight?" With this spirit there was never need to doubt the performance of all concerned.

The Queen arrives at Portsmouth Naval Base to welcome home ships of the Falklands Task Force.

Returning to Portsmouth with the Queen and Prince Philip

Commander-in-Chief, Naval Home Command

The Falkland Islands Task Force returns
H.M.S. VICTORY DINNER
Wednesday 6 October 1982

The Commander in Chief, Admiral Sir James Eberle GCB	HM Ships
Captain M E Barrow ADC	GLAMORGAN
Captain J J Black MBE	INVINCIBLE
Captain H M Balfour MVO	EXETER
Captain P G V Dingemans	INTREPID
Captain A Grose	BRISTOL
Captain C H Layman MVO	ARGONAUT
Captain D Pentreath	PLYMOUTH
Captain J F Coward	BRILLIANT
Captain J L Weatherall	ANDROMEDA
Captain N J Barker	ENDURANCE
Captain M G T Harris	CARDIFF
Captain D Hart-Dyke MVO	COVENTRY
Commander R J Campbell	HYDRA
Commander R I C Halliday	HERALD
Commander P V Rickard	PENELOPE
Commander P J Bootherstone	ARROW
Commander S H G Johnston	MINERVA
Commander N J Tobin	ANTELOPE
Commander P C B Canter	ACTIVE
Commander A W J West	ARDENT
Commander A C Lyddon	BACCHANTE

The war being over, I needed to turn my attention to a potentially difficult administrative problem that had arisen in relation to the required cuts in naval training, 'Slimtrain'. It was by now clear that the required savings could only be achieved by closing one of two major establishments in Portsmouth, the Torpedo and Antisubmarine School at HMS VERNON or the Gunnery School at Whale Island. The savings in each case were broadly equal. Although the very proper steps to bring to an end the tribal wars that existed between the various operational specialisations within the seaman branch had been implemented by the Principal Warfare Officer (PWO) scheme, tribal affiliations were still very strong. As a gunnery officer I was aware that, whichever way the decision went, I was on a personal hiding to nothing from one side or the other. In the event I was saved from this dilemma when it was discovered that it was not legal to sell Whale Island because the foreshore of the island belonged to the Crown and not to the Navy. VERNON had to go.

During the latter part of this year, I became increasingly aware that the case for maintaining a four-star admiral as CINCNAVHOME was increasingly open to challenge. My responsibility covered all the UK shore-side training establishments and other bits and pieces of our shore estate, other than the naval dockyards, which came under the control of the Chief of Fleet Support – a previous appointment of mine. CFS had under him three two-star admirals, the port admiral in each of the dockyard ports, who co-ordinated the civilian dockyard work and the uniformed support services. Under my command as CINCNAVHOME, there were three regional commands: the Flag Officer, Scotland and Northern Ireland; the Flag Officer, Portsmouth; and the Flag Officer, Plymouth. To me there was a clear case for combining the posts of the port admirals and the area flag officers who could then come under the direct command of the Second Sea Lord. The staff of CINCNAVHOME could then become integrated with that of the Second Sea Lord with considerable savings. The office of CINCNAVHOME could then be abolished. The resulting savings in the administration costs of the Navy might then be diverted into the operational field. I saw little point in one four-star admiral supervising three two-star admirals whose responsibilities could easily be absorbed by the port admirals.

In theory, CINCNAVHOME had responsibility for all the training establishments in terms of their proper implementation of a training policy, which was set by the Second Sea Lord. But, I was not responsible for the policy – only for its execution. This division of policy-making and policy execution is a long running saga in Whitehall and Westminster. In theory it is a sensible division. In practice, however, the boundary between the two is very diffuse. In my view it did not require the efforts of two separate senior admirals, one dealing with policy and the other with its execution. For this and other reasons, I became convinced that one of my objects should be to work myself out of a job. The expense of supporting the Commander-in-Chief, Home Command were also considerable – I had a large house, I had a barge and a barge's crew since I lived by the water, I had a considerable number of supporting staff officers, a large domestic staff, which I had tried to reduce but without success. I was told that if I reduced these billets other shore-side billets would have to be found for them in order to preserve an acceptable ratio of sea service to shore service in these branches.

In pursuit of my aim to provide reductions in the administrative costs of the navy (the tail) in order to provide additional money for the operational fleet (the teeth), I wrote a letter in January 1982 to the First Sea Lord proposing the termination of the office of CINCNAVHOME. The appropriate responsibilities being taken on by the area flag officers. I had previously written to him expressing the view that our training structure was too large and that we needed to take radical measures to reduce it. The latter proposal was not well received since he wished to retain as many four-star and two-star posts as possible in order to maintain flexibility in the pattern of succession for senior officers. Effectively the responsibilities of CINCNAVHOME have later been combined with other responsibilities. My proposal at the time when the defence budget was under severe pressure remains in my view a very sensible one, as has been borne out by subsequent reductions. I was just a few years too early in trying to get it accepted.

CINCNAVHOME did however have one additional role that provided an enjoyable opportunity for inter service activity and support. Together with my army and air force counterparts, we formed the Commanders-in-Chief (Home) Committee responsible for security within the United Kingdom. However, in my view, it generated little of value. In practice, any naval home security responsibilities fell to the three naval area flag officers. Furthermore, at that time the threat to internal security was almost negligible – and it was sometimes difficult to find items to fill the agenda of our meetings. But I nevertheless thought that it was useful to get ourselves together once in a while. On one occasion, when the agenda was very thin, I suggested to my army opposite number who was also a keen hunting man that our next meeting should be in the hunting field. Our only problem was that we could not get our airforce colleague to sit on a horse. We told him that he wasn't required to go up to 40,000 feet – 15-hands would do. John Stannier and I were not to be put off and we managed to find some brave group captain who was prepared to act as the Home Air Commander for the day when we met with the Tedworth Hounds. We had a good day and at the end of it I had no idea where we were but made quite clear that navigation on land was the responsibility of the army not the navy. I seem to remember that it took us quite a long time to get back to where our horsebox was waiting at the meet.

Towards the end of the year I was told that I would be relieved early in the following year. Not long before I had been summoned to London to lunch with several members of Mrs Thatcher's close entourage. I realised that I was being given the 'once over' treatment. The conversation ranged over various major defence issues including nuclear policy and the question of the cost of frigates. Whilst I was fully confident about the justification for my views I was also aware that they were unlikely to coincide with those of the Prime Minister, and in her book I was probably classified as 'not one of us'. I was also aware however that I was on the Chief of Defence's short list as his favoured candidate for one of three top positions. The first was First Sea Lord; the second was Chief of Defence; the third was as Chairman of the NATO Military Committee. I was not surprised that Margaret Thatcher's choice as First Sea Lord was John Fieldhouse who had won the South Atlantic war for her – and was an excellent choice. I was also not surprised that she might well be reluctant to change the practice, which had previously existed for a long time, that the Chief of Defence was taken in turn from the service chiefs of the Army, Navy and Airforce. On this occasion it was the Army's turn. The choice for the chairmanship of the NATO Military Committee lay between nations and a good friend of mine, a Dutch general, Cor de Jager, was a strong candidate. I had also made clear my view that the relations between the NATO Council and the Military Committee were such that the Military Committee's deliberations carried little weight within the Council. I thought there was much room for improvement; although I realised that certain of the NATO Council members would not view this with equanimity. Therefore, it did not surprise me that when I was asked to see the First Sea Lord, I was told that the only position he had to offer was that of Vice Chief of Defence Staff. This did not appeal to me, not because of the likely next Chief of Defence Staff, a soldier whom I knew and respected, but being 'vice anything' would not be my choice. I was therefore to retire from active service early in 1983 at the age of fifty-five, after having had the privilege of Flag rank for some thirteen years.

Before I handed over my command to Admiral Sir Desmond Cassidy in January 1983, I sent off a final 'whiz bang' to the First Sea Lord expressing concerns over the adequacy of naval staff training and the Navy's attitude to staff work. In my view, the result of this was that, at the higher level, our expression of the 'naval case' often lacked depth and intellectual rigour. This received a characteristically warm and supportive response from John Fieldhouse, sensibly pointing out that making such improvements would not be easy. Change seldom is. A few days later, I left HMS VICTORY in a horse-drawn carriage to take my farewell leave and resettle into a new life.

I relinquished my role as CINCNAVHOME and left active service in the Royal Navy sadly but without regrets. I had been extremely fortunate and successful in a career that I had greatly enjoyed. I had held to the beliefs that I believed to be important without compromise and regardless of the personal consequences. I was fit and active, with time for another life – although I had no clear idea of what I wished to do next. For my six weeks resettlement 'course', I chose to take my horse to the Royal Marine stables at Lympstone, ostensibly so that I could learn more about stable management. In practice, it also provided me with the opportunity to hunt four days a week, mounted or on foot with my beagles.

Almost as soon as I had settled down to my life on the farm at Holne and was beginning to be able to provide more support for my wife Ann, I was seduced by an invitation to do a lecture tour in the United States. As a result of my contacts with the English Speaking Union, I was asked to undertake a six-week engagement in America speaking on NATO. It was an opportunity that I found not too difficult to accept. My tour started in New York and went on to Cleveland, Ohio, and then to Omaha in Nebraska. I began to get concerned about Omaha because almost everyone in New York to whom I spoke about my itinerary said, "But why are you going to Omaha. *Nobody* ever goes to *Omaha.*" In the event, I was hosted most warmly there, as I was in Pittsburgh and elsewhere. I was asked to speak on the radio at a number of very small country radio stations, several of them run by a 'man and a boy' from a small shack. In this Midwestern rural environment, I did not expect my interviewer to be particularly enthusiastic or knowledgeable about NATO. It is of course not difficult for any professional radio jockey to think up the first one or two questions on almost any subject. But having dealt briefly with the first 'Good morning – welcome – what is NATO all about these days?' type question, I was very pleasantly surprised that the follow-up questions were almost always knowledgeable and penetrating. I was happily impressed.

My next appointment was in Denver, Colorado where I was due to speak on a Friday evening at a large and well-attended ESU dinner. I felt mildly embarrassed to find that I had been given priority over a visiting British junior trade minister who was present. So I took particular care to be both informative and amusing. I was certainly generously received. In conversation after dinner, one of my hosts asked if I had ever been to Denver before. I told him that I had been *through* Denver on a number of occasions on my way to nearby Aspen – but I had not before been to Denver.

"You must come to Aspen in the winter for the skiing, I imagine." "No. I am usually there in the summer for international conferences at the Aspen Institute. I don't actually ski. I spend all my spare time at home in winter, hunting." "Oh, we're hunting on Sunday," he said. Perhaps rather pompously I responded, "No, not hunting with a gun like you do here – I mean hunting foxes with horses and hounds." "Yes, so did I. We had our point-to-point last week – and Sunday is the last day of our season. We hunt coyote."

Some rapid adjustment to my planned programme saw me on Sunday morning sitting on a horse wearing a cowboy hat and boots at a meet of the Arapaho Hunt. It wasn't exactly like a day with a pack of English foxhounds – but it was of enormous fun throughout - and I was again made most welcome.

My next and last port of call was to Arizona. My host and hostess met me at the airport. At their home, I was also greeted by three Welsh corgis. I happened to know a little about this breed, because my elder sister in England had bred several corgi champions. My hostess, Margaret Bohannon, who had been born in Wales, told me that she also had recently acquired four couple of hunting beagles. I did not at first let on that I had been hunting a pack of beagles in England for some twenty-five years. When we went out to see the hounds in their run, she told me that she had not yet had the courage to let them out, since she had cottontails (rabbits) on her property – and she did not know whether or not she would be able to control them. I then owned up and told her that from my long experience, the longer she left them shut in, the more difficult they were likely to be when they were let out. I volunteered to take charge. Fortunately the hounds understood English hound language, and we successfully walked them out and returned them without incident.

After a few days, and another large ESU dinner and various calls, I was sorry to have to leave without seeing them hunt, whether it had been either a cottontail or a jack rabbit (American hare). We have since kept in touch and exchanged visits. One of the two of my own Britannia hounds that I drafted to the Paradise Valley Hunt distinguished himself by trying to kill a rattlesnake. Thanks to a rapid injection of anti-snake-bite serum, he survived.

I returned to England and Village Farm ready to face my new life, whatever that might be.

Commander-in-Chief, Naval Home Command

Fundraising for the "Mary Rose"
Dinner in Nelson's Great Cabin, HMS Victory

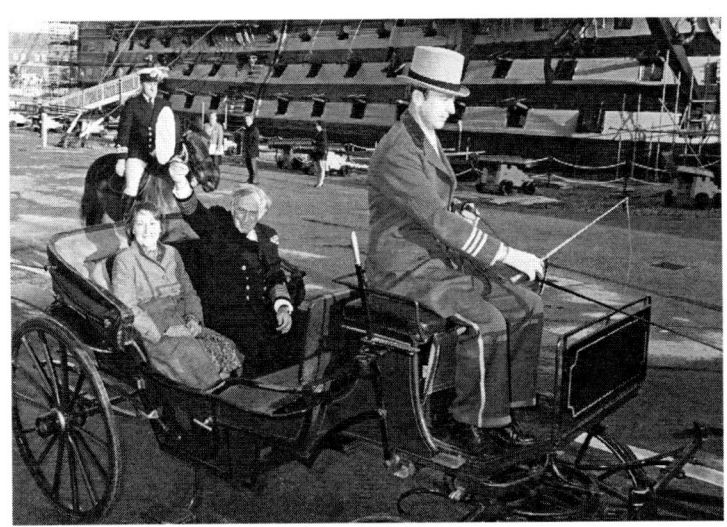

Ann and I leave HMS Victory

Chapter 4

The Royal Institute of International Affairs

"Diplomacy - The art of letting the other man have your way."
                                                                    Anon

When I got home from my NATO lecture tour in America, I was far too busy in catching up with the farm and trying to get myself and the Britannia Beagles ready to start autumn hunting again, that I had little time to give serious thought as to what I was now going to do for a living. I played with several suggestions such as joining the professional after-dinner speaker circuit – but that did not really appeal to me. Nor did I think that I could afford to take on the mastership of a pack of foxhounds, an idea that had for many years been running vaguely through my mind. Then one evening, the phone at Village Farm rang, and Robert Belgrave, a Shell Oil man whom I knew, asked me if I would like to be considered as a candidate for the directorship of the Royal Institute for International Affairs at Chatham House, a post that was becoming vacant in the new year of 1984.

I knew little about Chatham House. However, international affairs sounded interesting – perhaps an extension of the ancient sailor's dreams of having a wife in every port. I responded in naval fashion, "I don't know, sir; but I will find out." It did not require a great deal of research to tell me that this would certainly be of considerable interest – and that there was likely to be strong opposition. I came across a *Times* diarist reporting that amongst possible candidates were a former Permanent Representative to the United Nations, a distinguished former ambassador to Washington, a well known senior member of the Foreign Office, a very well qualified MP of high standing, and "a retired admiral whose name is not widely known even by me". An academic, well known in naval circles, and known for his feisty comments, was reported to have said that if it is an admiral, then it must be Jim Eberle, "He's the only admiral I know who can read and write."

I soon found myself called to interview. The chairman of Chatham House was Lord Harlech, a distinguished diplomat and former ambassador to the United States. He asked me where I thought that the Royal Institute fitted in to the governmental and non-governmental world of international politics. I responded that I thought it was particularly important that, in cases where governments found it difficult to talk with other governments due to doctrinal differences, as was the case with the Soviet Union and most of eastern Europe, that independent institutes should be able to assist in filling this void. There was thus a strong need for widely based research into doctrine and independent political and economic affairs.

I readily accepted the offer that quickly followed my interview. I was both surprised and delighted, and agreed to start on the 1st of January 1984, subject to my absence on Wednesdays for the first ten weeks for which I had already committed myself to hunt the beagles in Devon. So began another fascinating phase of my life.

The Royal Institute of International Affairs was founded in the aftermath of the First World War. British and American diplomats attending the Paris Peace Conference got together in Paris at the end of May 1919 to discuss, in the light of the causes and the outcome of the Great War, whether the more coherent study of international questions had a role to play in the future conduct of international relations. One of the conclusions was that there was a need for the academic and scientific study of the theory that governed the relations between nation states. At that time, there were effectively no departments of International Relations at universities on either side of the Atlantic. In London steps were taken to establish a new independent institute in Britain that would devote itself to such international study. An Institute of International Relations was started in Horseferry Street in Westminster. Some three years later, the institute was able to move into 10 St. James's Square. The house had been built and used as a private residence by Sir William Heathcote (1693-1751), a prosperous merchant. It had also housed three prime ministers, William Pitt, Earl of Chatham (1708-1778), Edward Stanley, Earl of Derby (1799-1869) and William Gladstone 1809-1898). Chatham House subsequently received a Royal Charter in 1926 and became The Royal Institute of International Affairs.

In America, it transpired that the embryo of such an independent institute had already been established prior to the beginning of the First World War. Additional resources were therefore made available to it and the New York Council on Foreign Relations was born. Both institutes grew in stature and independence during the inter-war years.

During World War II, Chatham House effectively became an adjunct of the Foreign Office. This proved an important and valuable resource for policy makers. Some of the staff and research material was moved to Balliol College in Oxford. It built up a substantial book and press cutting library, including British and foreign newspapers, which became much valued by the Institute's members and academic researchers. The Institute also organised courses in international relations for officers of the armed services.

Following the end of the Second World War, and the establishment of the United Nations with its vision of a 'new world order', departments of International Relations were introduced into a number of the new British universities. In addition to their role in the teaching of international relations, they provided a new independent research capability in matters of foreign policy that previously had been largely confined to the Royal Institute under the leadership of such distinguished academic figures as Kenneth Younger and Andrew Shonfield. Traditionally, some government funding had been made available to Chatham House to support such independent research. However, under Margaret Thatcher's government, such financial support became more directed and limited. This posed problems of the Institute's independence. It increasingly had to turn for funding to the business community and charitable foundations.

Fundraising was always a difficult issue. We employed a number of professional fundraisers, all of whom seemed to live on their nerves, which were often very near to the surface. Perhaps this is a fundamental requirement for members of this profession? It is a profession in which the Americans are far more skilled and practised than the British. I spent many hours with one of our fundraisers, an American, making the round in America of potential high worth donors. On one occasion, we visited a very well known American philanthropist from whom we had high hopes of a substantial donation. I opened as usual with a spiel about Chatham House and its transatlantic connections, to be followed by our fundraiser who started talking about particular projects and funding needs. Our host listened carefully and then, clearly, in my view, said 'no'. Our fundraiser tried again. He got the same polite response. He tried at least four times more, each time with an exactly similar response. As we departed, I said to our fundraiser that I had become very embarrassed because he had clearly said 'no' at the first attempt and had not changed his mind throughout. I feared he was going to throw us out. I think I would have done so. "That's the trouble with you Brits," he responded, "You give up too easily."

As I began to come to grips with the research programme as a whole, I sought gradually to move some of the responsibilities for research funding from the centre to the individual programmes. Inevitably, some research programmes found this more difficult than others. It was very difficult though for any of the programmes to find adequate funding to cover their contribution to the general and central administrative costs of the Institute. This devolution of responsibility for research funding also had its down side; effectively having to provide much of their own funding made it less easy for programmes to work very closely together. Such close internal research co-operation was a characteristic of Chatham House's work that was both internally and externally much valued.

A major central cost for the Institute was that of the libraries. These were in two parts. The well-stocked book library, with a highly professional staff, was much used and valued by our members and by our own and outside researchers. The other part was the press cutting library. This had been started in World War II to provide the Foreign Office with ready reference to national and worldwide reaction to the progress of the war. In its heyday, the staffs were reading, cutting and filing more than twenty national and foreign newspapers. Following the war's end, this number had gradually to be reduced as the process of maintaining the essential reference service was time consuming and expensive. We tried very hard to maintain the quality of this well-recognised service; but inevitably, we were forced by costs to cut fewer and fewer newspapers. Nevertheless, we were able successfully to transfer responsibility for the custody of this nationally valuable back collection to the British Library.

My predecessor as Director of the Royal Institute of International Affairs was David Watt, a highly distinguished journalist in the field of international affairs, who had been at Chatham House for five years. Soon after leaving the Institute he was sadly killed in an unfortunate accident. Management and leadership had not perhaps been his strong points, and it was clear to me from the start that the Institute was in decline in financial terms and in influence – morale within the house was not high. To restore the Institute's financial health, we had first to rebuild the Institute's standing at home and in the international field. Chatham House had to prove its worth if it was to pay its way.

In domestic political terms, the Institute's position had no affiliation to any party. Its research task, which I regarded as one of our two primary tasks, was aimed at examining policy issues with a view to informing government, politicians and the general public of the implications of various courses of action. Our other primary task was to keep our members and the public informed on international developments. This non-party position suited me well; since as a serving naval officer, I had steered well clear of any party affiliations. I was certainly not apolitical, as I held the view that military policy or action taken outside the context of its political environment has little meaning or legitimacy. However,

Chatham House had some Liberal traditions and I found myself surrounded by those of strong and active Liberal domestic political opinion. Indeed two of my principle senior staff were later to be appointed to the House of Lords as peers in the Liberal Democratic Party.

It was not easy to preserve a non-partisan position. The Labour party was moving left and the Thatcherites were challenging the political consensus. When the Prime Minister had doubts as to whether the Institute was on 'her side' or not, and did not want to listen even if it was, it made it difficult to promote a broader cross-party debate. There were those whom we found it difficult to persuade to come to speak at the Institute, because we were hopelessly 'establishment' – whilst we were frequently being asked to field speakers from the American 'new right' who were close to the Reagan White House. One senior Central American figure whom we had to speak was described by a distinguished British journalist as "one of the smoothest drug smugglers to walk in and out of the White House." You can never win them all.

My initial priority, having visited all the Institute's departments and talked with all of the staff, was to review the research programme. This was, I believed, the key to proving the Institute's worth. Sitting at my desk on almost my first day in the office, trying to familiarise myself with the depth and breadth of the research programme, the telephone rang. A voice said, *"This is the Canadian Broadcasting Corporation. We are getting martial music from Moscow and we think that Mr Andropov, the Chairman of the Supreme Soviet, has died. We await confirmation but will ring you again shortly to seek your opinion on the succession."* I immediately sought out the head of our Soviet programme to ask his advice on how I should reply. He was not available. I went round the Institute's offices to find someone else who might be well versed in such matters. I could find nobody. Moments of minor panic came over me as the phone in my office rang again to confirm the death of Mr Andropov. Somehow I was able to drag up the name of a possible successor, Mr Chernenko. When asked about him, I replied that we knew little, other than that he was one of the old guard and that it was unlikely that the change of leadership would result in any major change of policy. It was my good fortune that this turned out to be correct and it was not long before the death of Mr Andropov was confirmed. The leadership then came into the hands of Mr Chernenko who lasted barely twelve months before he also died. His successor was Mr Gorbachev, who was to lead fundamental changes in the Soviet Union. Soviet affairs thus rapidly came to the top of our research priorities.

A major attraction to both corporate and individual membership of the Institute was our lecture programme, for which the Institute had a substantial and well earned reputation. During my 'watch' at Chatham House, apart from Margaret Thatcher, there were few major international figures that did not speak at the Institute. The list included the President of the United States, who spoke at the London Guildhall, the Princess Royal, Mr Mitterand, President of France, Mr Gorbachev, General Secretary of the Soviet Union and the Prime Minister of Japan. The format at the Institute was for a thirty-minute presentation followed by thirty minutes for questions by invited press and Institute members. There was only one occasion when this was in danger of going awry. The speaker was Mrs Jean Kirkpatrick, then the US ambassador to the UN Security Council. I was in the chair. Despite confirming the format with her, after forty minutes of her thirty-minute oration, I could see that she was only about half way through the written script from which she was reading. After I had passed her two appropriate notes about her timing, she continued unabated. After a further five minutes she was still in full flow and I had to bring down my gavel. She was not best pleased.

Most speakers kindly provided a copy of their curriculum vitae to our meetings' programme secretary, Mrs Joe Statler. They were often several pages long. On one occasion, when I had asked one of our younger and less experienced members to take the chair, I said to him in advance that in introducing the speaker, there was no need to read out the full list of the speaker's appointments and achievements because they were very widely known – and our audience wanted to hear the speaker – not the Chairman. Thus briefed, he introduced our speaker with the words; "We are delighted to welcome our distinguished speaker today. As the Director has told me, his past is so well known that the less said about it the better." This was not entirely what I had intended.

Economic policy was clearly at the heart of much of the Chatham House's work. Economics however was not my strong suit. It was therefore with some trepidation that I faced one of my first personal challenges in my very early days at the Institute. It had been agreed by my predecessor that Chatham House and the well respected National Institute for Economic and Social Research (NIESR) would together contribute to a single volume setting out the strategic economic landscape. William Wallace, our director of studies, came to me to say that we were not prepared to proceed with this joint project because the contribution being made by the NIESR was not of sufficient quality to share the covers of a volume published by Chatham House. He explained to me at length where the difficulties lay which I struggled to understand. I was finally convinced. I said to William, "OK, what you want me to do now is to go to the director of the NIESR and tell him that their contribution is not of sufficient merit to be published under Chatham House covers?"
"Yes, just that."
"One final question. Do we know who in NIESR the author of this particular piece was?"
"Yes. It was the director."
"So you want me go and visit the director, whom I have never met before, to tell him that the piece he personally wrote does not match the standards of Chatham House?"
"Yes please."
"Thank you very much!"

I had the feeling that the academics in our Institute were giving me my first test. I am glad to say that I survived it and even remained on subsequent good terms both with the NIESR and its director.

I was very fortunate and privileged in my early days at the Institute to receive an invitation to attend the annual Bilderberg Conference held in Sweden. This was a private gathering which provided me with the opportunity to meet some thirty top political and academic leaders from around the world. This brought home to me the very high regard in which the Royal Institute of International Affairs was held. It also helped to open the door to me, as its Director, to a quite remarkable number of national and international organisations and conferences both as a participant and a speaker.

One of my first overseas visits was to South Africa as a member of a Chatham House team headed by our chairman Lord Harlech. We landed at Cape Town where we were greeted by a strong delegation from the South African press. Much to my surprise, Lord Harlech put me in to 'bat' first. I do not remember the exact question but it was of a highly political and sensitive nature regarding the British government's attitude to apartheid. In my naval career when abroad I had always left such questions to be answered by the ambassador. I was now in the hot seat. I tried to appear not to be flustered, which I was. However, somehow inspiration came to my aid and it all passed off very easily. My part role as a Foreign Office diplomat had begun.

It was a great sadness when not long after, Lord Harlech was killed in a car crash. His appointed successor was Lord Richardson, previously the governor of the Bank of England. One of my first tasks was to organise a visit to Washington of top British business leaders, which was to include a visit to the White House, the Congress and prestigious Washington personalities. It was hard work; not least in getting sufficient British businessmen to commit themselves firmly to the programme and its costs. Inevitably there were uncertainties. However, I was fully in favour of accepting a degree of risk in this respect before confirming the arrangements. My new chairman was totally against accepting any uncertainty. The visit was called off. He was soon to be replaced by Sir Christopher Tugendhat with whom I had a very close and harmonious relationship for a number of years.

I was able to build on the excellent relations with appropriate Foreign Office staff, whom I held in high regard. However, the views that I personally expressed were not always in strict accord with government policy. On such occasions I tried to make clear that I was speaking on a personal basis and that I did not represent the British government – or indeed the Royal Institute - but was speaking on my own behalf. Being the *Royal* Institute, however, some people both within and without government did not understand this. On one occasion I was sent for by the Permanent Secretary to the Foreign Office to remind me that, when speaking abroad, I must make it clear that I was not speaking to government policy. I was able to assure him that, on occasions when there was room for misunderstanding, I tried to do just this; but not everybody wished to accept it. We parted good friends. I never discovered what it was that I had said, or to whom I had said it, that was the cause of this 'demarche'.

In the six years of my tenure as Director of the Royal Institute, and thereafter, I found myself closely involved with a series of high-level international networks in all parts of the world – The Ditchley Foundation, The Anglo-German Königswinter Conferences; the Anglo-Soviet Round Table; the UK Japan 2000 Group; the International Institute for Strategic Studies; the US East West Institute for Security Studies. I found myself invited to attend, and often to address, conferences around the world, including Washington, Boston, Barcelona, Pittsburgh, Colorado, Moscow, Frankfurt, Potsdam, Munich, Amman, Dresden, Stockholm, Helsinki, Halifax (Nova Scotia), Hong Kong, Tokyo, New Delhi, Kuala Lumpur, Rome, La Paz, Basle, Bardejov in eastern Slovakia, Yerevan in Armenia, and Pontignano in Italy. I was pressed to visit Botswana, Angola and Mongolia, but much as I would have liked to have gone, the Institute in London was very properly too demanding of my time for me to be able to accept.

In Washington, the Royal Institute's standing was high. In June 1985, a Chatham House reception, hosted by the British ambassador, Sir Oliver Wright, was attended by many influential American personalities including the former US Secretary for

"Fire Power" at the Royal Institute, Chatham House
Henry Kissinger, US Secretary of State, Prime Minister Nakasone,
President Mitterand, Sir James Eberle

With Mrs Thatcher at No. 10

Defence, James Schlessinger. At the institutional level, our relations with America were also good and we were able to work in close harmony with the New York Council on Foreign Relations, although our ways of working were very different. At Chatham House, we would take what we believed were important issues, would research them and in due course present our conclusions, often in the form of a published Chatham House paper. The New York Council did not normally indulge in such in-house research. It tended first to invite a member of the 'great and the good' to address a meeting at the Institute to express his views on a particular international problem – and then to follow up by encouraging a public debate on the issues that had been raised. Indeed our in-house research staff was considerably larger than that of the New York Council. When I had joined the Institute we had about ten full-time researchers. Five years later it was about three times this number. This was not empire building. It was both a reflection of the growth of the international agenda and recognition of the increased standing of the Institute that enabled us to attract greater research funding.

Despite the good relations between Chatham House in London and the New York Council on Foreign Relations, at the government level Anglo-American relations were often under some strain, not least with regard to the conduct of the cold war. At the top level, the Ditchley Foundation's weekend UK-US conferences did an enormous amount in serious study of such international political, security, social and economic problems from a transatlantic point of view. As the decade progressed, the conference schedule increasingly involved the attendance of a small number of participants from other countries, thus reflecting a wider European and global viewpoint.

The Foreign Office conference centre at Wilton Park also made a significant contribution to discussions of global problems with delegates, often of a working-level, from all parts of the world. A foil for the immensely popular and valuable high-level conferences held at Ditchley Park was provided by the small but influential conferences held in America by the Aspen Centre for

Humanistic Studies set in the mountains of Colorado. At one of these that I attended, which concerned security and space issues, the chair was taken by an Assistant Secretary of State for Defence much respected for his scientific knowledge. In the audience was a senator not unknown for his aggressive politics. After the coffee break, the senator commented, "Chairman, your chairmanship of the last session was quite the worst performance from the chair that I have ever heard." The chairman responded, "Gentlemen I wish you to know that that was quite the nicest thing that the senator has ever said to me." Even so the conference continued in good spirit and much good sense.

At the lower end of the spectrum of learning, a great deal was being done by American universities in bringing students from America to summer schools in Britain during their vacations. However, there seemed to be a gap between about the ages of twenty-five to forty that was a very important formative stage for those who were, or were likely to be high achievers in their chosen field. In May 1982, following an initiative by Nick Butler, a young research Fellow at Chatham House, discussions had taken place in London on the subject of establishing some new form of regular contact amongst Britons and Americans, similar in style and purpose to the annual Königswinter conferences with the Germans. This idea attracted wide endorsement. Getting this initiative off the ground required funds – and these were not easy to come by. A visit to Washington found the Americans supportive – but without obvious enthusiasm. However enough funding was raised to allow the project to proceed – a project that sought to foster individual friendships and professional relationships between young 'pretenders' in the UK and the US.

In Britain, the project came to the attention of Sir Charles Villiers, a former head of British Steel and subsequently director of the British Industrial Reorganisation Corporation. Early in his life, Charles had been a student at New College, Oxford. In 1934 he was standing in the quad of his college when, across the hallowed turf of the lawn strode a large man who, on approaching him, thrust out his hand and said in a strong American accent, "Van

Dusen". That was the start of a lifetime's mutual friendship during which they exchanged letters in every week of the year. Lewis Van Dusen became an American lawyer and rose to the top of his profession. Charles believed deeply that that friendship was of immense value to both his personal and business life. They both agreed that they wanted to create an environment in which potential future leaders from both sides of the Atlantic would have the opportunity to make such lasting friendships. With the help of colleagues on both sides of the Atlantic, particularly Lord Carrington and Isadore Scott, a very generous donation from the Pew Foundation in Philadelphia provided funding for the first three "Successor Generation" conferences. It fell largely to Chatham House with the great support of Maxine Vlieland and her specialist conference experience to get started.

The first conference in 1985 took place between twenty young Brits and twenty Americans at a small conference centre at Middle Aston, near Oxford. It was a modest beginning, but was undoubtedly a success. We had appreciated in the planning that choosing the right participants would be very important, and that it would be necessary to try carefully to match the two sides. In Britain and America, a substantial nationwide trawl was made to ensure that participants were chosen from the full spectrum of society and professions, with as wide a range of interests and expertise as possible. On arrival, we divided the two teams into three sub-groups for their discussions. The first sub-group addressed issues related to international security; the second to international economics; and the third to social issues. These groups became colloquially known as bombs and rockets, cash and carry, and the bleeding hearts.

In a private summing up after the conference, Charles put his finger on a fundamental difference between the British and American cultures. He said, "On the American side there were sixteen doers and four thinkers – on the British side, there were fifteen thinkers and five doers." The following year's conference took place in Philadelphia. Lessons from Middle Aston in regard to the selection of participants had been well learnt – and this return leg was also an undoubted success, as was the third conference in Scotland.

The two advisory boards were now faced with the problems of the longer term. How was the project to be administered and funded? The founding fathers committed their full direct support for a further two years. After that this responsibility had to be taken on by the alumni. If that was not achievable, then perhaps the project was not worth proceeding with. Twenty years later the project, now renamed the British American Project (BAP) continues to be highly successful, there now being alumni of several hundred members in each country. Individual personal and professional relationships flourish, with annual conferences that are popular, relevant, exciting and fun, providing a corporate loyalty to the central theme of the project – Atlantic partnership. What more could one ask?

One of the strengths of the Institute was our energy policy group headed by Robert Belgrave. The group tended to plough its own furrow but continued to grow in its influence. The suggestion then emerged that it should also encompass environmental matters. There was some reluctance in the group largely because it was already heavily loaded, and I pondered this issue for some time. I eventually decided to seek the views of our Chatham House Council that consisted of many eminent individuals. One of these was Sir Robin Ibbs who had previously been the Chairman of ICI. More recently, he had headed for Margaret Thatcher, the newly created 'No. 10 policy staff'. He was a man of few words and great wisdom.

Our council presented something of a problem to me because I found it difficult to find decisions to refer to them that were of a substance deserving of their consideration. In most of the areas in which I found that I needed advice I was always able to refer directly to the chairman and receive views with which I totally agreed. The matter came to such a head that, at one stage, I discussed with William Wallace, my deputy director, whether we might invent a problem to occupy council meetings. We thought that we might invent a letter from a deceased member leaving a large country house to the Institute in his will. The problem for the council would then be what to do with it. Do we sell it? Do we reduce our overhead costs by moving all or part of the Institute out of central London? Or do we convert it into a Chatham House conference centre? Or ...? The differing views of council members, and our council discussions, would then be endless!

A matter in which I did genuinely need outside advice from the council was that of a proposal to widen the remit of the Institute's energy programme to include environmental issues. At the next council meeting, this attracted wide discussion to which I listened with care. After an hour or so, my deputy sitting at my side, attracted my attention and said, "I see Robin Ibbs has just caught the chairman's eye. What he says will be worth listening to very carefully." Robin said, "Mr Chairman, any great company that in future does not pay careful attention to environmental issues will not remain a great company for very long." I did not need to hear any more; I had made up my mind. Thereafter we had an increasingly successful energy and environmental department.

Space was also beginning to play a major role in terms of scientific research and international security. The European Union, led by France, was having a significant impact on the part that the European Community should play in the European Space Agency on both these matters. The British were far from happy. In the space research field there was pressure towards a European project for putting a man into space. The British did not see this as a proper scientific objective. In the military field, the British were concerned that the French were seeking to challenge American domination in satellite surveillance, with major implications for the NATO alliance. At home, the Government were seeking to limit the funds being made available to our own national space centre.

At Chatham House, we were asked to produce a seminal piece on British space policy for publication. I was well acquainted with a number of the British scientists involved in this field from my earlier connections with the missile research programmes at Farnborough. I also knew a little about space. The head of our

Chatham House European programme, Dr Helen Wallace, knew a great deal about policy-making. Working together we produced a Chatham House paper[4] that attracted considerable favourable comment. In the National Space Centre's view, it would have been of even greater value if we had been able to publish it a year before. Nevertheless it seemed to have some influence on our government policy makers. It was certainly the best paper that had ever been written by a British admiral (in partnership) on British space policy. I was able to make this assertion with great confidence since it was the only such paper ever produced by a British admiral. A colleague, commenting favourably on the paper, told me that he thought that it was very well written, and that he found it difficult to discern which parts Dr Wallace had written and those that I had written. This was fair comment because Dr Wallace produced the major part of the policy thrust. I certainly learned a great deal from her about the broader issues of government policy-making.

Another area of policy with which I found myself increasingly closely involved was that dealing with our relations with Japan. In 1978 Prime Minister Jim Callaghan had written to the Japanese Prime Minister suggesting that we need a closer relationship across the full range of political, economic and social issues. The result of this was the formation of a highly successful UK Japan 2000 Group whose affairs are recorded in chapter eight.

The early 1980's, when I had been at the highest level of naval and NATO command, I had seen the peak of the cold war – the Russian invasion of Afghanistan, the deployment on both sides of new medium-range nuclear armed missiles, the Polish civil unrest, the recently elected US President Reagan's declaration of Russia as "the evil empire", the shooting down by the Russians of a Korean civil air liner; and the Falkland Islands war. All served to produce an era of growing East-West tension. The second half of the decade, the time at which I was fortunate to be at Chatham

---

[4] *British Space Policy and International Collaboration (CHP 42) ISSN 0143-0000*

House, saw the genesis of unprecedented change in the international system – the collapse of Soviet led communism, the fall of the Berlin Wall and the restoration of freedom to eastern Europe, the rise and fall of the Japanese economy, the emergence of an Asian Pacific community, the development of the European Union; and the emergence of the USA as the one global superpower. These were the years of the emergence of globalisation, fuelled by extraordinary advances in technology, especially in the field of electronic communication.

For me, these months and years in the Institute seemed to pass all too quickly. It was a period of change in the international system of a depth, scope and speed probably unmatched in history. It was the time for building the new west European community and for dismantling the Soviet domination of Eastern Europe. It was the time of the ending of the cold war, symbolised by the breaking down of the Berlin Wall, the dissolution of the Warsaw Pact and the collapse of Soviet-style communism in Russia. It brought to the fore fundamentally new questions about the future.

In a speech at Chatham House, George Robertson, later to become Secretary of State for Defence and Secretary General of NATO, referred to this time as providing a "bonfire of the certainties". In a letter to *The Times* (April 27, 1987), I myself concluded with regard to our relations with the Soviet Union, "We stand at a moment of great opportunity. We have good reason to be sufficiently confident in our strength now to move gradually and safely from a policy of containment to competition and from confrontation to co-operation." Eighteen months later, following a visit to Moscow, I wrote in similar vein to *The Daily Telegraph* commending Mr Gorbachev's latest unilateral move in terms of conventional arms control, "Mr Gorbachev's move is much less a 'gift horse' than a new joint opportunity to move towards a less confrontational East-West relationship. How the West responds will be a major factor in determining the future behaviour of Mr Gorbachev and his like-minded colleagues."

There were those, like myself, who looked forward to a new and kinder world order in which there would be less armed conflict. National security was becoming increasingly interdependent and defined more in economic, rather than military, terms. This was indeed, the era of the "peace dividend" and major reductions in our defence programmes and expenditure. There were others who took the opposite view, fearing that following the removal of a global nuclear threat, action by the United States as the one remaining superpower, could release inherent global tensions that would lead to a more 'conflictual' world. By the end of the century, it was I who had been proved wrong.

In 1989, I had very happily renewed my contract as Director. However, personal circumstances took hold. In late 1987, my wife was diagnosed with ovarian cancer. I took a short period of absence to be with her, but very sadly she died in the following spring. I soon came to realise that without her support at my home in Devon, I was not going to be able to continue to lead the Institute in the way that I believed to be necessary with the hectic life, in London and abroad, which was involved. It was therefore with deep regret that, in due course, I asked the Chairman if he would begin the process of seeking my successor. The process was completed in January 1991 when Professor Laurence Martin, who had had a strong academic background in the study of defence policy and had more recently been Vice Chancellor of Newcastle University, took over as Director of the Institute. This was a very sad day for me in saying farewell to a staff, who at every level, from top to bottom, had given me their full, generous, friendly and effective support.

In November 1990, I had the great privilege of being invited to preach the Armistice Day service at Canterbury Cathedral. The precentor, a former naval colleague, Rear Admiral David Macey, kindly provided for me the script of the previous year's sermon by a senior military officer. Having read it, I had to say that I hardly understood a word of what it was about. He responded, "I shouldn't worry about that. Neither did the vast majority of the congregation."

I based my own address on my previous experiences of Hiroshima, Korea and the Falkland Islands' war to recall the motto of my own gunnery branch of the Royal Navy that reminds us of the paradox "Si vis pacem, para bellum". If you want peace prepare for war. I remembered in particular the reaction of my father, who suffered the horrors of World War I, when, in September 1939, he heard the Prime Minister's announcement that we were again at war with Germany. I finished my address with the words:

"We must ask the younger generation to remember that, whilst rightly looking to the future, they should not forget the past, for it is the supreme sacrifice of those who have gone before them whom we remember today, that allows us to live in an open and free society in which the individual has the power of choice. That power of meaningful choice for good may still be limited – although we need to be aware that removing these limits may increase the likelihood of choice for evil. We should have confidence in their choice; for without that, the sacrifices of the past would be in vain."

In December 1990, and following a farewell dinner in Chatham House at which I was deeply honoured by the presence of many distinguished political and academic guests, I had had the privilege of delivering my valedictory address to the members of the Institute, entitled "The Security Interests of Western Europe". I began this by examining the proposition that we had reached a time when we needed to try "to impose a new structure on the way that we tended to think about security and defence in the new and novel situation in which there is no longer a readily identified enemy." It was just over ten years later, that a terrorist attack on the twin towers of the World Trade Centre in New York initiated the "war on terrorism" and launched the world into a new era of insecurity that defies the normally accepted definitions of war. I address these issues in my final chapter.

I still found myself very much involved in the international field, however, and was determined that I should not lose touch with the Institute or its splendid and very loyal staff and disappear like a 'puff of smoke'. I believed that we had had a very happy 'ship' and I could never forget the loyal support that I had had from every level of the Institute's staff. I was therefore particularly delighted when it was agreed with the Chairman, and the new Director, whom I had known personally for many years, that I would continue working from Chatham House, and under its auspices, with some of the major projects with which I had been particularly associated. These included the high level personal relations with the Soviet Union, the UK-Japan 2000 Group, the British American Successor Generation Project, the Anglo-German Königswinter Conferences, the Conference on Security Cooperation in the Asian Pacific Region, the Anglo-Argentine Conference and various other smaller international commitments in India and Latin America. These commitments kept me fully occupied and involved me with the Institute staff at all levels and a great deal of international air travel.

After I had announced my intention of standing down as Director of the Institute at the end of 1990, I was invited by Paddy Ashdown, leader of the Liberal Democratic Party whom I had known briefly before, to join a small group of senior military officers to advise him on operational matters concerning the impending Gulf war. When I came to Chatham House in 1984, I was without any political baggage. As a serving naval officer I had steered well clear of any party affiliations. I held the view that military policy or action taken outside the context of its political environment had little meaning or legitimacy. I was certainly not apolitical – but as a serviceman I regarded myself as being non-political in a party sense. I was aware that there were very few senior military officers who paid allegiance to the Liberal Democratic party, I therefore accepted. We had a number of meetings with Paddy which went well.

I was also invited by the BBC to act as a TV military advisor. One late evening I found myself on studio duty with Jonathan Dimbleby. Soon after midnight we received a report of an Iraqi rocket attack on Tel Aviv. This was a serious escalation of the conflict. However, it rapidly became much more serious when

CNN started reporting that this was a nerve gas attack. I was dubious and cautioned that we should await some confirmation from another agency before going live on this on the BBC. In the event, my caution was justified. What happened was that as soon as the rocket struck, those nearby noticed unusual fumes coming from the crater and assessed this as nerve gas. The medical attendants treating the wounded, thus injected atropine, an antidote to nerve gas; and confirmed this action very correctly by marking a large letter A on the forehead of each of the casualties. (This is similar action to those who have been treated with morphine for their injuries who are marked with a large M). When the media arrived they saw wounded being taken away with the letter A on their forehead. They therefore assumed nerve gas. As it turned out, the fumes from the incoming missile were not nerve gas but the residue of the rocket's unburned propellant.

Jonathan was most grateful for my advice of caution and asked on what I had based this. I told him that being in a studio such as we were, with information coming in rapidly from many sources, was like being in a warship's operations room during an action when information is flowing in rapidly from many quarters, some of it is accurate, some of its is false and all of it is very confusing.

After the end of the war, Paddy asked me if I would speak for the Lib Dems at the forthcoming general election. My initial response was to say no since, although I thought I knew a considerable amount about international politics, I was neither deeply interested nor knowledgeable in national political issues. After a little pressure, I agreed to speak only on military matters.

During the election campaign, my phone rang one evening and I was invited to go to north Somerset to speak on behalf of the Lib Dem candidate, where there were a number of local military issues, particularly concerning departments of the Navy. I was not initially enthusiastic but since I had made various contributions to the Liberal Democrat defence policy stance, I succumbed to pressure. I turned up at the appointed place and time where there was a small media presence. I was immediately pressed upon and asked why I was appearing for the Lib Dems. I told the surrounding press pack that I had read with interest the Liberal Democratic defence policy document (I carefully avoided saying that I had contributed to writing it) and thought that it made sense and deserved support. I was there to express that support. Following a little more questioning which went well, an attractive young TV lady asked me if I would do a piece to camera. I agreed.

"Why?" said my interviewer, "are you here?"
I repeated my earlier statement.
"Are you a member of the Liberal Democratic party?"
"No, I am not a member of any political party."
"What are you then?"
"I am a floating voter."
"How can a floating voter speak for the Liberal Democrats?"
"Well, what would you expect an admiral to be?"

Game, set and match.

Despite the brevity of this political encounter, Paddy Ashdown asked me to continue giving advice on defence issues after the election, since the party planned to produce a revised policy document. I agreed to help. Several months later I found myself at the Liberal Democratic headquarters in Smith Square at a meeting of the top Lib Dem Policy Committee with Paddy Ashdown in the chair. I was not entirely enamoured with some of the concepts and their phraseology. At one point I was challenged by the question, "Well, why can't we say that?" Somewhat sharply I replied, "Because it's not true." Having got my way I began to feel guilty because I was not even a member of the party. To be laying down the law to the policy committee on what they could and could not say seemed a bit much. At an appropriate break, I slipped out and went down to the ground floor where I asked a helpful secretary to make me a member of the Liberal Democratic Party. I feared that if some members of the policy committee found out that I was not even a member, there could be a certain amount of brouhaha.

I continued my membership of the Liberal Democratic party in order to support an initiative by a former naval colleague, Brian Friend, in the formation of a pressure group within the party to give emphasis to rural issues. This was the Liberal Democratic Forum for the Countryside (LDFC). Despite some financial problems, the forum has continued under Brian Friend's leadership to be a successful lobbying group on rural issues including field sports. Having attended at least one party conference, and become more acquainted with the ways of domestic politics, it became increasingly clear to me that the Lib Dem party was neither particularly liberal nor democratic. In the 2002 general election, whilst I was still living in South Devon, I had become increasingly disillusioned with all the political parties and their way of conducting politics. My local constituency had been Conservative for many years. The challenging Lib Dem candidate was female, young and virile. However, it seemed that the thrust of her campaign was aimed at personal criticism of the sitting candidate. This was not a way of conducting politics with which I could agree. I therefore had printed and circulated some 20,000 copies of a leaflet that in effect said - if you are disillusioned with the conduct of all the political parties, what do you do? Please don't abstain. Vote for an individual, not a party – an individual whom you judge will best support your own personal interests and those of the constituency. In my own case, I revealed that on that basis I would vote for the Conservative candidate, who went on to win. The local Lib Dem committee then fired me from the party, confirming my view that they were neither liberal nor democratic.

The following years were full of change, interest and some new commitments for which Chatham House was the ideal partner. One of these was an invitation to a European-Latin American security conference taking place in La Paz in Bolivia. It was a long haul from London but it was invitation which I welcomed as it was a region and an area of policy which was new to me. At the conference, I personally found that the discussion was mostly somewhat lacking in reality and substance. Unfortunately, I intervened at one stage to make the suggestion as to how matters might be improved in the field of European-Latin American security. My suggestion was warmly received – with the almost inevitable result that I was invited to take the necessary actions. When I had returned to London, I rather regretted that I had opened my mouth! I am not sure that the outcome of my efforts was particularly successful but they certainly occupied a great deal of my time.

Prior to my visit to La Paz I had attended a conference in Barcelona. On arrival I studied my brochure in which it said, "Catalonia is a country ...". I had thought it was merely a province of Spain with Barcelona as its capital city. As I quietly investigated this, I found myself increasingly surprised at the degree of independence from Madrid and the national government which Catalonia enjoyed. This brought to my mind the problem of Gibraltar, where I suspected that there was no knowledge of such a relationship within Spain.

As the turn of the century was approaching, I decided to run down my commitments in London, and to take my leave of Chatham House. My final mission, also on behalf of the FCO, was to Beijing to prepare the ground for a British initiative to form a new quasi-governmental group, similar to the UK-Japan 2000 Group, for the discussion of matters of mutual concern. I returned with a very positive message. For the first time within Chatham House, however, I found myself in conflict with a new member of staff recruited for his knowledge and experience of China. My personal view was that he was not suited to take on a task at this level of diplomacy. This was a matter for the Director, not for me. I did not feel that I still had the energy and drive to resolve this matter and bring this important project with the Chinese Government to fruition. Having also become involved in an unpleasant personal matter with someone that I had tried to help, unwisely perhaps, it was time for me to 'hang up my hat' and retire from the international scene for the third time.

There was though still one invitation that I could not resist. In April 1999, I was invited by the BBC to visit Washington for the NATO Summit and 50th anniversary celebrations, and to do a live

TV commentary for the opening ceremony. The Voice of America Radio also enlisted my services. It all seemed to go very well and I much enjoyed it. It provided the evidence though that confirmed that it really was time for me to go. When I got home, a good friend of mine told me that a colleague had said, "Did you see the old admiral on television yesterday? I think the last battle he must have fought in was Trafalgar!"

It really was time out – and I was ready to go.

Chapter 5

Europe

"Don't take life too seriously. You'll never get out of it alive."
Bugs Bunny

The future of Western Europe and the development of the European Community clearly lay at the heart of the Royal Institute's programme. The Institute was fortunate indeed to have as our Director of Studies, Dr William Wallace, a leading academic in the field of European Studies. A major element in our European research programme was the need to further the contacts between Chatham House and our fellow institutes in western Europe – the Deutsche Gesellschaft für Auswärtige Politik in Bonn (DGAP) under the leadership of Professor Karl Kaiser; L'Institute Français des Relations Internationales (IFRI) under the leadership of Francois Thierry de Mombrial; the Italian Instituto Affari Internazionali (IIAI) headed by Caesare Merlini. I much enjoyed the task of successfully establishing close personal relationships with each.

To set the background to the new European programme under the highly capable direction of Dr Helen Wallace, we arranged a small conference at Chatham House to review the decision by the British Government in 1955 not to join in the negotiations over the Treaties of Rome that established the European Community. It was a fascinating occasion with a number of the key players attending the conference. It became quite clear that the Treaty of Rome had been regarded in political circles as being the basis for 'a customs union'. Customs matters were not a concern of the Foreign Office; they were a concern of the Board of Trade. One of the senior civil servants who attended a final meeting to determine whether or not Britain should join in the negotiations over the Treaty of Rome said that he well remembered that meeting. There were representatives from many of the government departments concerned with trade matters – and at the end of the table was a single representative from the Foreign Office. He did not utter a word throughout.

At that time, government ministers also showed little interest or understanding in what was happening in Western Europe. Britain therefore decided not to join the negotiations of the Treaty and thus failed to have any significant influence on the way that Western Europe was to develop economically or politically. Following the failure of the European Free Trade Area (EFTA) and Britain's late entry to the Community (Common Market) in 1972 under the government of Ted Heath, it remained an uphill task for Britain to acquire influence over the conduct of European economic policy (The Common Agricultural Policy, the Common Fisheries Policy or the fixing of Europeans internal and external tariffs). During the EEC entry process, the British electorate were repeatedly assured that the Community was a beneficial trading agreement that in no way involved a loss of essential national sovereignty. The pressure for an ever closer political union was difficult to resist, however, even for Margaret Thatcher after she became Prime Minister in 1979.

I was soon made aware that our relations with Margaret Thatcher, at least on Europe, were not as close as I would have wished, a difficulty that we shared with the Foreign Office with whom our relations were strong and professionally founded. The Foreign Office was under no illusion as to the political implications of this agreement for our national sovereignty. Not long after I had taken over as Director, I was kindly invited to a formal dinner at 10 Downing Street in honour of Richard von Weizsäcker, the former mayor of West Berlin and President elect of the Federal German Republic. It was a very pleasant and relaxed occasion with the guest of honour making a very thoughtful after-dinner speech about the future of Europe and its leadership. He told that, because of two world wars in Europe, Germany could not take a lead – and nor could France, effectively because 'France was France' – so here was a perfect role for Britain. In responding, Margaret Thatcher made a short but justifiably complimentary speech about Richard von Weizsäcker. However she totally ignored his challenge about Britain's role in the future leadership of Europe. After dinner, when it was time to go, I went to thank the Prime Minister for a very interesting and enjoyable evening. I added:

"Prime Minister, you have not been to the Royal Institute for some time (I was not sure that she had ever been to Chatham House). We would be honoured and delighted if you would come to address members of the Institute. Perhaps you would consider addressing Richard von Weizsäcker's question as to Britain's role in the future leadership of Europe?"

She smiled and responded, "There are some questions that are better not asked. There are some matters that are better not addressed."

I replied, perhaps rather unwisely, "In that case Prime Minister, if that is your and your government's policy towards Europe, would you like to come to Chatham House and say so?"

She then put her hand on my arm in a very motherly way and added, "That was just two lines, not a speech."

This was of course a complete 'brush off'. But she did it in such a way that I could not reasonably have been upset. It was clear to me that as far as she was concerned, neither Chatham House nor its new director was "one of us".

The fundamental policy issues in Western Europe related firstly to the future of the political and economic structure of Europe – and secondly to matters of security. In the former case, pressure for the further development of the community, mainly from continental European countries, became increasingly overlain by the conflict between the role in European security of NATO and the Western European Union (WEU). The major difficulty of this issue was the position of France. Having earlier withdrawn from the military structure of NATO, the French Government were constantly pressing for a greater role for the WEU. This matter had never been resolved and continues today in a somewhat altered context, a problem being driven on by French opposition to the US-UK invasion of Iraq and the expanding role taken upon itself by NATO, firstly in the Balkans; and now outside Europe in Afghanistan.

In the political and economic field, we at the Institute, had a difficult hand to play. Mrs Thatcher was very reluctant to surrender national political and economic policy to the growing power of the European Community, a route which our own political analysis strongly favoured. The Foreign Office was also in a difficult position in that many senior Foreign Office officials were also firm believers in further 'Western European political development', not least in the light of political developments in Eastern Europe. Mrs Thatcher's reported comment on the British governmental system at that time was to the effect that the Home Office dealt with domestic issues supporting our own people in Britain – whilst the Foreign Office was there to support foreigners. Nevertheless there was a wider driving force in the economic field, that of globalisation, and free trade. The independent Trade Policy Research Unit which had functioned for some years was overtaken by events and folded through lack of financial support. A degree of that mantle fell to Chatham House.

In these fields, we found ourselves in close harmony with our fellow institutes in France (IFRI), Germany (DGAP) and Italy (IIAI) and proceeded with a number of initiatives involving our common interests, for which we had support from the European Commission. On one occasion this provided us with an opportunity personally to brief Jacques Delors in Brussels on the thrust of our joint work and to seek some financial assistance from the Commission for it. Such 'federalist' ideas were not welcome by the Thatcherite wing of the Conservative party and were accompanied from time to time by almost vitriolic attacks on the Institute from certain sections of the national press for developing links with the Soviet leadership. My own personal contacts at a high level in Moscow earned me the title in *The Times* of 'the red admiral'.

In the bilateral field, the interchange of ideas and opinions with the Germans was particularly strong within the context of the

Königswinter conferences[5]. This annual series of bilateral conferences has grown from very modest beginnings in 1950 when twenty British practitioners visited Germany, a divided state still struggling to cope with the aftermath of the Third Reich and the war, so as to assist in the social reconstruction of the country. It developed rapidly into an annual meeting of informed individuals of influence in a very wide range of disciplines, not only discussing bilateral matters, but also the great issues of international politics. These meetings, to which I was privileged to contribute during my time at Chatham House, were characterised by the free and frank exchange of views within groups of both like-minded friends and opponents. The undoubted great success and value of Königswinter, including the establishment of a 'Young Königswinter', has provided a formula for the establishment with many other nations of similar round table and bilateral groups.

At the transatlantic level, an American institute became one of the leaders in the non-governmental process of East-West discussions. This was the Institute for East-West Security Studies (IEWSS) run initially from New York by John Mroz but later expanding its administrative reach to Prague. I was invited to join the board. At the government level in Western Europe, West Germany took the lead both with Moscow and East Berlin in measures that might lead to the re-unification of Germany.

In the Cold War climate in which we still existed at that time, the questions of arms control remained a central East-West issue. Inevitably, the position of the United States Government was crucial and such formal discussions were almost entirely conducted at inter-governmental level. This did not, however, deter the many independent experts on both sides from expressing their personal views in public. Nevertheless, Independently led conferences on East-West issues were of particular interest and important.

The fall of the Berlin Wall in 1989 was to be the climax of East-West detente. I was in an aircraft flying to America when this

---

[5] *See "40 Years on – Four decades of the Königswinter Confernce"*

happened. I had not expected such a dramatic event so soon. When I landed in New York and watched on TV these dramatic events – the first step in the process of dismantling the East West divide in Europe – I felt somehow rather cheated not to have been able to watch it live. I felt a little bit like the golfer, accompanied on the course by his wife, who did a hole-in-one. He was elated, although somewhat chastened by his wife's comment, "Darling that was wonderful – but I wasn't watching. Could you do it again, please?"

Two of their IEWSS conferences that I attended come especially to mind. The first was a meeting held in June 1991 in the east of Slovakia at Bardejov. I was fortunate in getting a lift in a private jet from an American industrialist for the first part of the journey from London. This still left us a two-hour drive by car to the conference location. We passed along very primitive roads through a somewhat featureless agricultural landscape that was being heavily cultivated. Yet I saw not a single tractor nor agricultural vehicle – nor were there many cars on the road. There were also not many men to be seen wielding agricultural instruments – the workers on the land were almost all women. The scene merely brought home the backwardness of nearly all forms of livelihood behind the Iron Curtain. This only led to re-enforcing our belief in the need to further develop a meaningful East-West dialogue.

The other conference that springs particularly to mind was that held at Potsdam in East Germany two years later. Potsdam was, of course, the centre where the post World War II division of Europe was initiated, dominated by the three giants of the war, Stalin, Roosevelt and Churchill. It was in the middle of these discussions that Winston Churchill had to stand down, to be replaced at the conference table by the newly elected British Prime Minister, Clement Atlee. He had just come to office as a result of the 1945 British election. One cannot but imagine the impact on Stalin of this dramatic change.

As part of our conference programme arranged by the East German authorities, we were invited to go to Berlin to a reception at which we would meet the members of the East German Politburo. The reception was held in an excessively grandiose, Germanic-style, government building. The members of the Politburo formed a reception line and after some delay we all shook hands with them. At the time I remember thinking that this line-up was quite the most depressing collection of seedy looking officials that I had ever before had the misfortune to meet. I particularly remember the East German Economics Minister. He had only one arm and a patch over one eye. This did not seem inappropriate.

Another conference on East-West relations held in East Germany in 1992 was organised by the IISS and attended by several European and NATO foreign ministers, including Hans Dietrich Genscher, the West German Foreign Minister and his East German counterpart. Whilst inevitably the principle speeches reflected the deep division between East and West marked by the Berlin Wall, it was for Hans Genscher a particularly emotional occasion as his own birthplace was nearby. Even so, it was clear that we were beginning to make progress towards an ending of the cold war. Perhaps because the Nordic balance of East-West relations was somewhat less militarised than that in Central Europe (a theme that had been led by Norway's Defence Minister, Johan Jorgen Holst, a former academic) the Norwegian Foreign Minister, Theovold Stoltenberg, had been invited to address the conference. He spoke in the following vein – that having listened with great interest to the views of the East and West German Foreign Ministers, he wondered what contribution the Foreign Minister from a small Nordic country could make to this discussion; particularly in relation to the role that young people could play in the process of reunification. "I believe we must extend the Eurorailer project," he declared boldly. He then went on for some little time about the value of the Eurorailer. His audience was a little bemused. He then stopped, paused and said, "I don't believe that most of you know what the hell I'm talking about." He was quite right. He then went on to explain that the Eurorailer was a project that permitted young people to travel by train across the whole of Europe on extremely low fares.

There was no doubt that he had made a 'veritable hit' at the meeting. I discovered that he was accompanied by his extremely attractive daughter and arranged with her that on my return to London, I would have a T shirt made emblazoned with the words "I am a Eurorailer" which she promised to present to him on his forthcoming birthday.

The process of reducing East-West tensions proceeded step by step, steps that from the East were usually led either by Poland or Hungary. It was at Budapest that we put together a security conference of officials and academics that was, for the first time ever, attended by senior serving military officers from NATO and the Warsaw Pact. The Warsaw Pact side was led by General Lobov, then Commander-in-Chief of the Soviet group of forces in Germany. The first morning was a little stilted but seemed to be going well. The meeting was conducted in English with simultaneous translation available in other languages. General Lobov, however, seemed to spend most of his time talking to the Soviet staff officers who surrounded him. We optimistically thought that his staff was briefing him on the implications of what was being said. At lunchtime one of our most helpful Hungarian supporters came to us and said that General Lobov was very disappointed in the conference so far. He had thought that he was attending in order to answer questions. But nobody had asked him any. He was becoming disillusioned and was threatening to leave the meeting. We all agreed that this would represent a serious step backwards. We thus spread the word, particularly amongst the academics, that we must address questions to the General.

Accordingly, early in the afternoon, an academic, not well versed in the delicacies of such discussion did address a serious question to General Lobov. There was immediate concern in the Soviet camp whilst they worked out a response. The General eventually produced a typical communist-type statement. The academic responded in polite western university-style that he thought that this reply was effectively a load of nonsense. There was consternation in the Soviet camp. It was clear that Soviet generals were totally unused to their statements being challenged. It took a lot of verbal manoeuvring to prevent an immediate walk-out. This meeting, whilst not resulting in a great meeting of minds, nevertheless did represent a small but significant step in the process of the disintegration of the Warsaw Pact.

The multinational nature of the IEWSS meeting and education programmes did not prevent bilateral East-West contacts with other institutes. In Chatham House, through John Roper, the head of International Security, we started to develop a relationship with an East German (economic) institute in East Berlin, Institut für Politik und Wirtschaft. What we did not know until much later, after the Berlin wall had fallen, that this was an institute with connections to the STASI, the East German secret police. At the request of the Foreign Office, an East German round table was established. It may well be that this had some bearing on a personal matter which happened some while later. I was not aware at this time that there had been some speculation on the possibility of STASI penetration of Chatham House with the names of several highly distinguished members and associates of the Institute being the subject of low level press comment.

I was not long retired from the directorship of the institute and was happily ensconced in my farmhouse near Blackawton, Devon, when my neighbour came to tell me that, earlier in the day whilst I was out, a gentleman had been roaming around looking for me. He would not say what he wanted and said he would come again the next day. I had no idea who this might be. As far as I was aware, I had paid my taxes and my bills. So there was nothing to do but wait for the next day. Not long after nine o'clock a well-dressed middle-aged man presented himself at my farmhouse door and asked if I was Admiral Sir James Eberle. I replied that I was and asked him how I could help. He introduced himself as the head reporter of *The Times* newspaper and asked if he could come in and talk to me about Chatham House. I said I was delighted to talk about the Institute. It was one of my favourite subjects.

He told me that there had been recent open access to the records of East Germany's secret police, the STASI. There were two sets of records that had been bought by the US after the collapse of the Berlin wall. The second set was in a high-grade code that they had not yet been able to decipher. However, the lower classification records indicated that there might have been a STASI spy at Chatham House. Did I have any idea whom that might have been?

I had no idea whatsoever since I had had a splendid staff, all of whom had my full confidence. He went on to say that included in this STASI file was at least one paper about naval affairs. I spent a long time going through, one by one, all my staff at the Institute. My only thought of a possibility was a young Dutch post-graduate student who had been with us for a while on a short attachment. We had strong suspicions that he had been responsible for the loss of money from the desks of members of the staff. Subsequently, I found that a considerable sum had been stolen from my own bank by means of a forged cheque. We were glad to get rid of him.

However, I had no reason to think that he might have been working for a foreign intelligence service. Clearly, however, the so-called spy had been sending back to Berlin documents from Chatham House purporting them to be classified. To me, this was ridiculous. There was nothing of a classified nature that we ever did at Chatham House. Indeed, one of the raisons d'étre of the House was better to inform the public of what was going on in the world. If 'our' spy had sent back papers from Chatham House, he had probably bought them over the counter at the door – for all our papers were on display and for sale. I was at some loss to explain the naval paper and asked the reporter if he knew the date of this paper. He said it was in the late 1970s. This of course was long before I became the Director.

We talked for a long time going backwards and forwards over all the ground when the reporter turned to me and said, "Has it occurred to you that you might have been the spy?" In view of our conversation I was rather taken aback and replied honestly, "No,

It hadn't ever occurred to me." He then referred again to naval matters and suggested that this pointed towards me. I responded that some people might add two and two and make it four. I meant of course to say make it five. Nevertheless I thought no more of it, and he departed with my thoughts ringing in his ears that the whole thing was ridiculous. If someone in London working for the STASI was sending back information of alleged security value from Chatham House, then he must have been pulling a very fast one on his East German spy-masters.

I was the therefore somewhat surprised when, on the front page of *The Times* the next morning, there was a rather fanciful report of our discussion written in such a way that an interpretation could have pointed in my direction. Fortunately the Foreign Office came very quickly to my support and released a statement to the effect that that the whole thing was ridiculous since Chatham House had no access to classified information. That, to my mind, was the end of the affair.

Some two years later my telephone rang. The caller was Dr. Anthony Glees of Warwick University. He, with official support, was writing a book on the history of the STASI[6]. He knew about my interview with *The Times* newspaper. He told me however that the high-grade STASI records had now been deciphered. I had had a personal file in these records. The file contained a copy of two passports of mine – one issued in 1975, when I had been serving in the Navy - and the other in 1985, when I was at Chatham House and in need of renewing my previous passport. An interesting fact was that my 'old' passport had not got the top of the front cover cut off – this is always done when a passport has expired. Nor were there any visa stamps in it although he knew that I had visited many parts of the world. However, this was not surprising to me since in the Navy one had no requirement to use a passport in any foreign port. The second passport, interestingly, also had no visa stamps in it although, by this time at Chatham House, I was travelling very frequently

---

[6] *The STASI Files by Anthony Glees. ISBN 0-7432-3104 -X . pages 278-280*

abroad and had always had my entry and departure into any foreign country, except the European Union, stamped by the immigration authorities. Dr Glees asked me if I could explain this. I could not. He asked me if I had any idea of who might have 'stolen' my passports and had them copied. I told him that they were normally kept in my drawer at the office but that I was very surprised that any one would have known enough to take them in the very short time between my renewal and my first foreign visit. The thought therefore was that perhaps the STASI had an agent in the passport office and had obtained photocopies from there. This at least seemed to me a plausible explanation and I could think of no other.

Our conversation then turned to the question of why the STASI had 'picked me up' in their high security records. This apparently had happened in the early 1980s. This of course was a time when we knew that the Russian KGB had initiated their biggest ever security review when President Reagan's 'Evil Empire' speech had alerted the Russian leadership to the possibility that America might be planning a pre-emptive strike on the Soviet Union. We discussed a number of possibilities. That was the time that I had had a number of disagreements with Mrs Thatcher over nuclear matters, including the replacement of our submarine launched deterrent, Poseidon. I had never discussed these disagreements with anyone else – and if this had indeed been the cause, it could point to a possible leak in the area of No.10.

It also transpired that the STASI had abruptly 'dropped' me some four or five years later. This was unusual in that they had not dropped several others who were picked up at the same time. I searched my memory for any possible reason why this might have occurred. The only possibility that we could find was that, at about that time, I had acquired a special close connection with the Security Service. I was of course at that time often travelling in Eastern Europe, and had contacts with a number of Iron Curtain diplomats in London. I told him that I had never before that moment ever mentioned this to anyone and certainly not to any of my colleagues in Chatham House. That could have seriously undermined my position there. The only conclusion that we could draw, if that was indeed the reason that I had been dropped, was some form of leak within the Security Service. This was all fascinating stuff and a total surprise for me - but it was now some ten to fifteen years ago and was thus 'history'. Apparently the relevant agencies that might have been able to help had better things to do than rake over the past. The matter now properly rests with more questions outstanding than answers.

The confusion of this period was well illustrated in a speech at Chatham House, by George Robertson, later to become Secretary of State for Defence and Secretary General of NATO, in which he referred to the European situation as being a "bonfire of the certainties"[7]. In a letter to The Times (April 27, 1987), I concluded with regard to our relations with the Soviet Union, "We stand at a moment of great opportunity. We have good reason to be sufficiently confident in our strength now to move gradually and safely from a policy of containment to competition and from confrontation to co-operation." Eighteen months later, following a visit to Moscow, I wrote in similar vein to The Daily Telegraph commending My Gorbachev's latest unilateral move in terms of conventional arms control. I wrote, "Mr Gorbachev's move is much less a gift horse than a new joint opportunity to move towards a less confrontational East-West relationship. How the West responds will be a major factor in determining the future behaviour of Mr Gorbachev and his like-minded colleagues."

There were those, like myself, who looked forward to a new and 'kinder' world order, in which there would be less armed conflict; in which national security was becoming increasingly interdependent, and defined more in economic than military terms. This was the era of the "Peace Dividend" and the government's Strategic Defence Review, with its emphasis on future expeditionary warfare.

---

[7] *Drawing on Tom Wolfe's successful book* –The Bonfire of the Vanities

However, I had seen the advent of nuclear weapons as having changed our thinking about the role of armed force as an agent of political change. As Mr Gorbachev himself phrased it, "One country's security cannot be obtained at the price of the insecurity of another." However, international terrorism had been a strong thread running through many of these later years of the cold war. Threats to western and particularly United States interests had been posed, both by state and non-state actors. The American response, as in the case of Colonel Gadaffi and Libya, was from time to time of a strongly military nature. In 1986, the American Sixth Fleet launched a series of air attacks on Libyan territory. I believed that such action was perceived by many Europeans as dangerously over-reactive. In an interview with *Newsweek* in New York in May 1986, when asked to review the European reaction to the American air attacks, I had said, "Europeans find it hard to see terrorism as an act of war. They see it as a challenge to their society, not a threat to their national sovereignty."

How wrong I was later proved to be in respect of Iraq, and, the unilateral abandonment by the United States of the policy of deterrence and its replacement by that of 'pre-emption', with almost no internal or external debate following the '9/11' attack on New York. I had hopes that the United Nations might now be able to play a more effective role in world affairs, as had been foreseen by its creators. It had never, however, been achieved; neither in international security terms, where the UN Security Council had a recognised role to play; nor in terms of international polity, where the UN Political Committee had established its own virtual and actual invisibility. There were others who took an opposite view – that the removal of the threat of local conflict escalating to superpower confrontation, and all the dangers that that could bring, would lead worldwide to greater, rather than lesser, regional instabilities and conflict.

In my valedictory address to the Royal Institute in December 1990 I raised the issue of how we tended to think about security and defence in the new and novel situation in which there was no longer a readily identifiable enemy. I discussed the impact that this would have on the US-Europe military relationship within NATO. Despite the eroding of East-West confrontation, many people in Western Europe still felt that their lifestyle, and thus their security, was threatened but that these threats were not of a military nature, nor could they effectively be confronted by the use of armed force. The newly perceived threats arose through the challenges of new technology, the uncertainties of social change, the fear of unemployment, the danger of environmental pollution and climate change, the rise of new diseases such as AIDS; and now, perhaps, BSE and bird flu.

In a seminal address by Professor Adam Roberts[8] he described the international situation as follows, "International law and society are still caught in contradictory principles. On the one hand the sovereignty of states and non-intervention in their internal affairs, and on the other hand human rights; on the one hand the equality of states and the other the special privilege of the five permanent members of the UN Security Council."

At this time I was strongly of the view that defence policy must be the servant of foreign policy – and that the geopolitical and historical differences within Western Europe were such that there was unlikely to be any natural alignment in foreign policy to the extent that it would form a coherent basis for an effective security policy that covered the United States and Europe. The possible alignment of Eastern European countries with Western Europe, having thrown off the yoke of Russian imperialism, would make this problem a great deal worse. This transatlantic alliance had of course been the very raison d'être for NATO in the light of the Communist threat from the Soviet Union and Eastern Europe. But that threat was now fast disappearing. In the future, what would NATO be for? At this time, I expressed publicly serious doubts as to its continuing effectiveness.

Despite the careful approach to the former countries of the Warsaw Pact by such innovative concepts as 'Partnership for Peace' and 'restructuring' of the alliance, this question continually

---

[8] *The Martin White lecture 1991 – 'A new age in international relations'*

raised its head. Fortunately perhaps, an answer came to be found in the case of the Balkan wars, that NATO was the 'only show in town' that could help America in the search for a new balance of power in the region, based on democratic ideals. That such NATO involvement required the abandonment of certain fundamental conditions of the original NATO Treaty, such as that NATO would never go to war unless attacked, were conveniently forgotten.

NATO was unable, and unwilling collectively, however, to play any part in the Iraq conflict. Opportunistically, though, it has been willing to take on such a role in Afghanistan, although with considerable reservations by individual countries as to the size and duration and tasks of their contribution. It can reasonably be said that, if military power on the ground in Afghanistan can provide the basis of a future coherent Afghani state, ruled by the principles of democracy, then the 'new NATO' will have won its spurs in the Middle East. What would then be the implication for European participation in the solution to the wider and longer-term Middle East security problems is not easy to predict.

Present indications do not provide cause for optimism in such an outcome in Afghanistan. Many of those who have had hands-on political and military experience of this region strongly believe that the creation of an Afghan Nation State ruled by democracy, in a region so deeply divided by tribalism and strongly controlled by local warlords, is highly unlikely in any reasonable timescale.

The NATO countries' commitment to maintaining forces in Afghanistan goes only as far as 2008. Unless, by that time, NATO forces have been able to achieve a demonstrable transition from a tribal and warlord dominated country to a working democracy, there must be strong doubts as to the will of NATO countries to maintain military forces in Afghanistan. This might well cause new doubts as to the future of the 'new NATO', the cohesion of any European foreign and security Policy, and the commitment to Atlantic security.

The future structure of international security was fundamentally changed following the Al Quaeda attack on New York on the eleventh of September 2001. The reaction of the US President was to describe this as an "act of war". Whilst it is an entirely understandable reaction, it has led to a serious confusion between the interests of national security and those of national territorial defence. War, as we have known it over several centuries, has been concerned with the acquisition of, or defence of, territory. The war on terrorism has no territorial limits. It represents a conflict between ideologies. An ideology cannot be changed by the use of armed force. Nor can the use of armed force be a means towards the establishment of a working democracy. The utterly mistaken decision for the joint US-UK attack on Iraq, the outcome of which can now only be rightly described as a disaster, is leading to a fundamental global crisis about the nature of war, its relation to security and its management within and between nations. The evolution of lasting stability in the Middle East region would appear unrealistic in the near future. This may unavoidably lead to a new discussion of the political, defence and security relationships between Europe and the United States. Statesmanship is called for – but if a statesman is described as a politician with strategic vision, it does not seem that, in these days, many statesmen are to be found.

I address these issues further in Chapter 9.

Chapter 6

Moscow and the Soviet Union

"Men with big canoes have big problems."
Old American Indian saying

I had come to Chatham House with the initial fanciful idea that, having spent my life dealing with defence and security issues at almost every level, I would not now again become involved too closely in security issues. There were two other prestigious institutes that dealt with such matters. The International Institute for Strategic Studies (IISS) dealt with international security from an international perspective and the Royal United Services Institute (RUSI), of which I was a one-time member of the council, dealt with British national security issues from a national point of view. It was a 'child' of the British Ministry of Defence. The later establishment of the Centre for Defence Studies at Kings College under the leadership of Professor Michael Clarke was a further step forward in relation to the study of national defence. But that left open the field of international security policy from a British point of view, which was the business of the Foreign Office and, to a lesser extent, the Ministry of Defence. However, with the Cold War at its height, this perspective could not be ignored. Fortunately I had on my staff John Roper, now Lord Roper, who was the editor of the Institute journal *International Affairs*. In his political career he had become well versed in defence issues and soon took over as head of the Chatham House research department dealing with international security.

My first serious involvement in Russian affairs was to deal with a visit to London by their Deputy Foreign Minister, during which the Foreign Office had scheduled a meeting at Chatham House. My first question to the head of my Soviet Studies team was, "What is the agenda?" "That's entirely up to you," was the response. This was music to my ears. For too long in the senior levels of the MoD, a very strong political steer would have governed the agenda for any such meeting. Too often one saw on the brief the phrase, "On no account are you to make any response on the subject of ..." The agenda that I set for this meeting was fairly bland. But the meeting, attended by the Soviet ambassador and a representative of the Foreign Office went rather well, and I was surprised at the openness of the Soviet minister's responses. This meeting whetted my appetite for more; and I looked forward to establishing closer relations with our parallel institute in Moscow, the Soviet Institute for International and Economic Affairs (IMEMO). Together with the Soviet Institute for America and Canada (ISCAN), these two institutes provided major policy inputs to the Soviet Government.

I had not long to wait for an opportunity. In 1978, Prime Minister Jim Callaghan, sensing the difficulties of formal government-to-government contact had initiated with the Soviet leadership the establishment of an Anglo-Soviet Round Table (ASRT), for which the RIIA and IMEMO were to be the lead institutes. The UK membership of this informal non-governmental group, some twelve in number, consisted of prominent foreign, defence and economic policy representatives together with senior political figures. The group met annually alternately in the two capitals. The ASRT initiative was broadly modelled on the success of the bi-annual Königswinter talks that were set up in 1949 with the Germans. The ASRT was to set the tone for several more such non inter-governmental groups in which government representatives took part. They were well described as GONGOs – Government Organised Non-Governmental Organisations.

The first ASRT meeting, and my first visit to the Soviet Union, was to take place in Moscow in 1984. Together with my Soviet counterpart, Alexander Yakovlev, we would jointly chair the meeting, the agenda of which would cover a wide range of political, cultural, economic and security issues. I was a little nervous of this task bearing in mind the prominence of some of my British colleagues and my own position as a former senior NATO military commander. On this occasion, our group was led by Lord Harlech, the chairman of the council of Chatham House, a very experienced diplomat and former UK ambassador to

Washington. On arrival in Moscow, I found the atmosphere at the airport very close and rather intimidating. It was so very different to that of any of the many international airports that I had visited previously. However, we were well received by the deputy head of IMEMO, Oleg Bykov. Our hotel was equally intimidating with a floor lady – a large, elderly babushka (grandmotherly woman) who guarded all the rooms on her floor.

We were well looked after in Moscow and had the special pleasure of seats for the ballet at the Bolshoi, where the British were not frequently to be seen. There, we found ourselves closely attended by a very well dressed and attractive young lady. We were strongly of the view that she was probably linked to the KGB. As far as I am aware, however, none of us got any 'offers', and she disappeared off our screen at the end. So our views may have been uncharitable!

We were also flown by Aeroflot to Yerevan in Armenia in the southern Caucasus. This was a very different scene from Moscow, with well-stocked shops selling almost everything – even a motorcar - at a price. We were also taken to the opera for a splendid performance by a cast that had recently returned from South America. The director, whom we met, spoke good English. The centrepiece of our visit, however, was to the nearby centre of the Armenian Church, the cathedral at nearby Etchmiadzin. This is reputedly the oldest cathedral in the world. There we had an audience with the head of the Armenian Church, the Catholicus. He was very interesting and answered our questions in a frank and open way. We asked him about the Church's relationship with the Soviet regime. In essence, his response was of the nature that if we don't bother them, they don't bother us. When asked if the Church received any money from the Soviet state for the upkeep of the magnificent cathedral, he replied in the sense that they had to apply from time to time for building materials – but did not get money – adding quietly, "We don't actually need it."

The force of his remark soon became clear as we were shown round an extraordinary collection of very fine paintings, donated by members of the Armenian diaspora over many centuries. We were then taken to a small adjoining room where our guide, pulling aside a curtain on the wall, revealed a large, heavy steel safe door that he unlocked and opened. This in turn revealed a most breathtaking view of a large Armenian cross fashioned in gold, mounted on the wall and set in a fabulous background of precious stones. "This," he said, "was a present from the Armenian Church to the Armenian people." It was truly magnificent. Having carefully closed the safe door with its Chubb locks, he moved to one side and drew back a similar curtain on the wall to reveal an identical steel door. When the guide unlocked this we then saw an exact replica of the previous Armenian cross. The wealth represented by these two magnificent crosses was almost unbelievable - and certainly added reality to the Catholicus's remark on money, that they didn't actually need it.

The agenda of our first Anglo-Soviet Round Table meeting in Moscow had been well chosen. It generated little more than statements of well-accepted policies on both sides. We then came to the military situation. The Russian speaker was General Batenin, a two-star general in the Soviet armed forces and consultant to the Soviet Central Committee. The translation by the Russian interpreter droned on. It was remarkable how quickly one came to terms with 'Soviet speak'. But as I listened, I began to receive what seemed to me a somewhat familiar message. As he ploughed on I began to realise that what I was listening to was a story entirely similar to that which I could have received in Brussels by a NATO spokesman saying why NATO felt threatened by the Soviet Union – that Soviet power and influence was being extended throughout the world – that the capabilities of Soviet forces were increasing at an alarming rate – that these capabilities were increasingly offensive, and their progressively sophisticated weapons were being supplied from a growing Soviet defence industry base. Subsequently, as I gathered my thoughts and impressions on this session, it came to me that there was a remarkable degree of 'mirror imaging'– each side viewing the other as offensive and threatening.

For me personally, an important part of this visit was a long private discussion that I was able to have in Moscow with Alexander Yakovlev, the head of IMEMO, at their offices on the outskirts of the city. We discussed the problem of mirror imaging. Yakovlev had been the Soviet ambassador in Canada. He described to me the visit made to Canada by Mr Gorbachev who, at that time, had been the Soviet Agricultural Minister. This had been the first time Mr Gorbachev had visited outside the Soviet Union. Yakovlev described how much Gorbachev was taken aback by the general standard of living in Canada. He had had no idea that western economic development had permitted such an extraordinary rise in the standards of living, standards that were not to be seen anywhere in the Soviet Union. Yakovlev said that Gorbachev had found this visit not only a deep political experience but an emotional one as well. In the light of subsequent events this was to have a remarkable resonance.

I returned to London with the feeling that there was a great deal to be done to ease the problem of mirror imaging and that this could hold a key to further development of the Anglo-Soviet relationship.

Mikhail Gorbachev first came to London in 1984 in his role as Soviet chairman of the inter-parliamentary Anglo-Soviet Group. He met Mrs Thatcher whose response was to say, "This is a man with whom I can do business." One of the team that Gorbachev brought with him was Yevgeny Primakov, whom I had met at our Round Table meeting in Moscow and I had been much impressed by him. He was friendly and open and I would have been happy to make the same comment as Mrs Thatcher. Primakov introduced me briefly to Gorbachev, before Primakov and I returned to Chatham House. I found our discussions objective and encouraging for the future of Anglo-Soviet relations, despite the very high level of international tensions – for this was the time of the Soviet rejection of American offers of co-operation in a Strategic Defence Initiative (SDI); the further deployment of intermediate range nuclear missiles by both side in Europe, the

Soviet war in Afghanistan and the shooting down of a Korean civilian airliner.

It was in the spring of 1986 at a lunchtime meeting at Chatham House when a young British academic was talking about the outcome of the twenty-seventh conference of the Soviet Communist Party. In his conclusions, he said that he saw the seeds of substantial change in Moscow. The Russian ambassador was present, as was one of his staff, a young diplomat, Nikolai Kosov, with whom I had not infrequent dealings. He was very personable, intelligent and easy to talk to. I was not sure about his position in the embassy but he seemed to have remarkably close connections with the ambassador himself. I assumed he was a KGB officer. I was firmly assured by the appropriate UK authorities however, that he was not. At the end of the meeting, several of us, with Nikolai Kosov, were discussing the outcome of the meeting. Kosov said nothing to contradict the speaker's conclusion and I got the clear impression that he too thought that significant change was on the way. I was later to meet Kosov in the Kremlin in Moscow where he was holding office as an assistant to a senior member of the Politburo. He was equally friendly and forthcoming about the changes that were then taking place there.

On that occasion, I had found the inner sanctums of the Kremlin somewhat intimidating. It was difficult to get out of my mind the story told to me by Dr Joseph Luns when he, as Secretary General of NATO, was invited there for a meeting with the Politburo. As they were seated and before the meeting had started, a remark was made in Russian that brought hearty laughter from all round the table. When he asked what was the joke, he was told that it was nothing. However, Dr Luns refused to go ahead with the meeting without knowing what it was that they were all laughing about. Very reluctantly, he was told that one of the Politburo members had commented to the effect that Joseph was sitting in the very place that Beria had been sitting when he had been shot and killed. There followed a spine chilling account of what had

Foreign Minister Yvegeny Primakov (r) with President Yeltsin
Moscow 1990

then actually happened before Beria's body was smuggled out from the building in a rolled up carpet.

Whilst the prospects for change were fascinating, there seemed every probability that they would be very slow. We had not, however, foreseen the early demise of General Secretary Andropov; nor some fourteen months later, in March 1985, of his successor, Konstantin Chernenko. It had been reported that at Andropov's funeral, the British Foreign Secretary, David Owen, a well qualified doctor of medicine, having observed his body lying-in-state in the Lenin mausoleum in Red Square, had commented that he thought he looked in better health than his successor, Chernenko, whom he had just met.

Following the early death of Chernenko, it was not long before the Gorbachev era began to spring surprise on us all with his policy of Glasnost, freedom of expression, closely followed by his policies for economic reform, Perestroika. I became rapidly aware that both Yevgeny Primakov and Alexander Yakovlev had been taken as advisers into the Gorbachev camp, which was now clearly seeking fundamental change in the Soviet system.

Although in western eyes, the likely pace of change in the Soviet Union seemed uncertain, it was clear that our research within Chatham House called for higher priority and more resources. A programme was set up under the direction of an experienced and well-respected Soviet specialist, Alex Pravda, with funding support from the UK Economic and Social Research Council.

During our second Round Table meeting in London it was clear that fundamental change in the Soviet Union was well underway, a process in which both Primakov and Yakovlev were now deeply involved. I found Mr Primakov anxious to discuss the Soviet difficulties in achieving such fundamental changes which would extend throughout all levels of life in the Soviet Union. He asked me specifically whether I could help to get a team of western economists to come to Moscow to advise on the reform of the Soviet economic structure. This I passed on to the Foreign Office. I tried hard to persuade Primakov to come with me on a UK television interview to discuss the progress that we were making in our Anglo-Soviet relationship, at least at the non-governmental level. He was willing in principle to consider this but eventually decided, wisely perhaps, that he could not do so. He did not feel sufficiently confident that his command of the English language was adequate to ensure that he did not say something which could be construed in a totally different way to that which he had intended.

To broaden the interest level for the Russian delegation to the second ASRT meeting, we took them to Bristol for an evening at the theatre. One member of the Soviet team was an elderly, former GRU (military intelligence) general, Michael Milstein. He had been pronounced 'clean' by our relevant authorities. At dinner, he remarked to me that he had had three whiskies. There were four empty glasses in front of him and two more lined up.

The evening was to be followed by a farm visit near Bath on the next day. I had previously been shown a Soviet-style dairy farm during a visit to Hungary. It had a milking herd of four hundred cows and a labour force of about fifty people. The Duchy farm was milking one hundred cows with one herdsman and a relief milker. During the farm walk, our visitors' comments and questions brought vividly home the vast differences in style, substance and efficiency of farming Soviet-style and that on a Duchy farm in England.

At one time, Michael Milstein took me to one side and asked: "How is it that you can be an admiral, the director of a globally renowned international institute and also a farmer?"

I told him that I employed a farm manager.
"Oh, you must be a very large, rich and important farmer to be able to employ a farm manager."
"Certainly not. My farm is very small, is in a very beautiful area and I love it dearly. But it doesn't make any money."
"How then do you afford a farm manager?"
"I married her!" I replied – since it was my wife who ran the farm.

I had also mentioned to Michael that I had played tennis for the Royal Navy for many years. "Oh," he said "on your next visit to Russia you must play tennis," and he told me that he was head of the Soviet Forces Tennis Association. I was later able to take him to the All England Club at Wimbledon, of which I was a member.

I told him that I had never come across any tennis courts in Moscow.

"Ah," he said, "we have a very good club with courts for generals – only for generals."

"But I am an admiral."

"We make you a general."

I wondered quietly how a tennis club only for generals could be justified in the Soviet system. The hierarchy of the Soviet Union clearly looked after itself.

At our third meeting in Moscow which I chaired jointly with Yevgeny Primakov, the atmosphere was decidedly more encouraging than that engendered from our first meeting. At a private dinner à deux at one of the small and excellent restaurants in Moscow that were not available to the general public, we had a long discussion on progress in reform in Russia which was becoming ever more difficult. I ventured the view that it had been a mistake for Gorbachev to launch a programme of both Glasnost and Perestroika at broadly the same time. Glasnost, the freedom to speak freely, would be taken up without delay. But the economic changes implied by Perestroika would take many years to implement. I clearly remember Primakov's exact words in response. Leaning across the table, he said, "Jim, I know that – but it is more than my life is worth to say it." I found it a very emotional moment as I realised that he might well have been speaking literally.

It was not only at the level of the major institutes that we were beginning to make progress. A small independent institute based at Adderbury in Oxfordshire, the Foundation for International Security, was able to set up an informal exchange between Russian and British naval representatives through the efforts of its founder, Stan Windas, and supported by a British naval academic, Eric Grove. This initiative had been fostered by the success of more formal contact between the Russian and US navies in support of their 'Incidents at Sea' agreement. An earlier potentially dangerous close-quarters situation that had arisen between HMS EAGLE and a Soviet destroyer had added a British dimension. The Adderbury talks, which I attended, were undoubtedly worthwhile and in due course led to the formal recognition of annual trilateral naval meetings held annually in Britain, in Newport, Rhode Island and Petrograd known as the RUKUS talks.

At about this time in Moscow two new institutes appeared. The Institute of Europe was set up, initially under the direction of Sergei Karaganov, who was a newcomer to our Chatham House scene, but became a very useful contact. The other institute that came into being was the Russian Institute of National Security and Strategic Studies. It was headed by Sergoi Blagavolin, whom we knew well from IMEMO. It was not immediately apparent what influence these new institutes held in the higher levels of Soviet Government affairs, but the new directors certainly brought a new sense of realism to the East-West relationship.

At the level of the Anglo-Soviet Round Table, some wider progress could be noted. In the 1988 issue of the Soviet Military Review there was published two articles on military doctrine. One giving an account of my own views and one giving the views of a professor Andrei Kokoshin. He was deputy director of the Institute of the US and Canada Studies (ISKAN) – an important institute, headed by the influential Georgi Arbatov, and which rivalled IMEMO within the USSR Academy of Sciences.

I next saw Andrei Kokoshin when I met with senior Soviet officers at the Soviet Ministry of Defence to discuss strategic issues. It was several years since I had seen Kokoshin who by then had been appointed as the First Deputy Minister of Defence. He was the first civilian to hold such an appointment and I was horrified to see that he had aged tremendously in those few years. It was clear from the conduct of the meeting that, being a civilian and former academic, his views were neither acknowledged nor welcomed. Essentially he was ignored by his military colleagues. This perhaps gave substance to a later occasion when John Nott, the British Secretary of State for Defence, was asked to address the Senior Military College in Moscow. The first question that he was asked was, "What qualifications as a civilian do you have to be Minister of Defence?"

During our third Anglo-Soviet Round Table, I was also able to talk with Yakovlev about the very difficult problems that he was now facing in his new task of restructuring the relationship between Russia and the states of the USSR. It was an almost impossible task. All of the republics wanted independence from Moscow. Such a complete break-up of the Soviet Union was clearly not then going to be accepted by Moscow. I suggested that the problem needed more lateral thought - that Moscow needed a relationship with its neighbours somewhat akin to the British Commonwealth of Nations – and in a somewhat puckish moment, added that they would need to call it a communwealth. It was not very long afterwards that Moscow announced the formation of the Commonwealth of Independent States (CIS). I clung privately for some time to the fanciful idea that my remark may have contributed in some way to this, even though the CIS was not a great success in fashioning new working relationships in the political, economic or security fields. I was subsequently told, however, that the idea of some form of commonwealth had been circulating within the Soviet Foreign Ministry for some time before my talk with Yakovlev.

It was also in the margins of the third Round Table meeting in Moscow that I discussed with a senior Russian officer, General Batenin, a former Central Committee consultant, the policy of no first use of nuclear weapons (NOFUN). The Soviet Government had endorsed this policy – but NATO refused to do so. General Batenin argued that this demonstrated the offensive character of NATO's threat to the Warsaw Pact. I argued that 'no first use' was not a credible commitment.

"Let me give you a scenario. We are at a very high state of tension between East and West. Substantial measures of military readiness and reinforcement have been taken by both NATO and the Warsaw Pact. One evening, the head of the KGB goes very urgently to the Politburo and announces that 'cast iron' intelligence had been received that NATO was planning a pre-emptive nuclear strike from known nuclear bases in Western Europe against a Russian tank army now massing on the German border. You have the capability of taking out those NATO nuclear bases but only by the use of your own tactical nuclear weapons. The military assessment is that it is in your clear security interest to take them out now. Your political commitment is not to be the first to use nuclear weapons. I would not be confident that you would put your political commitment before your security interest."

There was no response.

Our British team for this visit included Conservative and Labour party politicians represented by Nicholas Soames and George Robertson. Before our scheduled departure for the conference I paid a brief visit to nearby Red Square with George Robertson. At one moment, he noticed me staring rather intently in the sky above the square. "What are you looking at?" he asked, "I was just observing the detonation point of the first nuclear strategic missile that would hit the Soviet Union in the event of nuclear war," I replied. On that chilling note we moved off for the start of the first meeting.

Nicholas Soames, being a member of the Churchill family, was made particularly welcome. At dinner that night he told a story of a member of the Churchill family, Randolph Churchill, who was not popular in London political circles. He was reported as having to enter a nursing home for an autopsy on a growth in his chest. It was suspected that this might be cancer. That evening at his club, Whites in London, when colleagues were gathered round the bar, Lord Camrose was tasked with ringing the nursing home to find out the state of Randolph's health. He spoke to the Sister who told him that an autopsy had been conducted and the result was that the growth was benign. Mr Churchill was fine and would be leaving the nursing home the next morning. On his return to the bar, Lord Camrose announced that the news was good and that the growth was benign. This caused a certain member to say in a loud voice, "Bloody stupid doctors. They've taken out of him the only piece that is not malignant." The Russians, who worshipped the Churchill family found it difficult to understand the humour in this.

On the Soviet side, the story was told of a Moscow citizen, exercising his new rights, who criticised the keeper of a butcher's shop for profiteering in the price of the sausages that he was offering for sale. "Look," said his prospective purchaser, "your sausages cost X roubles. Further down the road, the butcher's shop is offering sausages at half this price. How can this be right?" "Ah," said the shopkeeper, "It is simple. I have sausages to sell. Down the road he has no sausages."

There remained throughout the Soviet Union an astonishing extent of misconception about the West as can be illustrated by a piece in *Pravda* in 1987 describing the English officer:

> The English Officer is least of all, an officer. He is a rich landowner, house owner, capitalist or merchant and only an officer incidentally. He knows absolutely nothing about the army and the army only sees him on parades and reviews. From the professional point of view he is the most ignorant officer in Europe. ...The English officer is a beautiful aristocrat, extremely rich and an independent sybarite and epicure. He has a spoiled, capricious and blasé character, loves pornographic literature, suggestive pictures, recherché food, strong and strange drinks. His chief amusements are gambling, racing and sport. He goes to bed at dawn and gets up at midday. ...Military matters interest no-one and training in the army is left to the NCOs.

In London, I had the pleasure of a meeting with the head of the Soviet Armed Forces, General Ogarkov, who was visiting in response to a Foreign Office invitation. We met in my office at Chatham House, where I had mustered John Roper and a young Lithuanian who was working in the Institute and spoke fluent Russian. Amongst the small party that Ogarkov brought with him was the senior Air Attaché from the Soviet Embassy, a general with a lively and personable character, to act as interpreter. The occasion was relaxed and informal with nuclear weapon issues occupying much of our agenda. This was a positive and useful exchange of views, much enlivened by the Air Attaché's frequent misuse of the word "detergent" when he meant "deterrent".

The Yeltsin-Gorbachev coup in August 1991 and the announcement of the formation of the CIS changed the whole tempo of UK-Russian relations. In November of that year, I had been invited to Moscow at the invitation of Professor, and former general, Nikita Chaldymov, to take part in a high level conference under the title, 'The Armed Forces and Military Service in a Democratic State'. It turned out principally to be a discussion on the future role of the Zampolit – they were the political officers in the armed forces responsible for upholding and enforcing Communist party doctrine. In a Soviet warship the senior Zampolit had equal status with the captain. Communist doctrine was now out. What was the future role of the Zampolit? Very cleverly they had devised a new role; that of providing a personnel management and welfare branch for the Soviet armed forces.

The conference was being held at a former Party centre on the outskirts of Moscow. I was anxious to talk to Primakov, who, following the Yeltsin coup, had been made head of the KGB. I managed to obtain a telephone number for his office and spoke to his secretary. The result was an invitation from Yevgeny to lunch with him. He would send a car to collect me. In the light of my inability to speak Russian and the limited English of his office, I was not totally confident about the detailed arrangements. However, I believed that one of his assistants whom I did know would come and collect me at half past twelve. I waited at the entrance. Time passed. By one o'clock I was beginning to think that I had either the wrong day or the wrong time. By twenty-past-one I determined that if nothing had happened in the next ten minutes, I would 'throw it away'. At that moment a car drew up and his assistant jumped out apologising profusely for being so late. He said that they had been unable to find this place. Being a little cross, I responded somewhat testily that I hoped their foreign intelligence was better than their domestic intelligence. He smiled wanly and we jumped into the car and drove off at high speed. It was clearly a KGB car although we did not have an escort. The weather was vile with mist and heavy rain. Our route took us along the Moscow ring road. Anyone familiar with the Moscow ring road at this stage would have regarded its condition as more like a rally track through the Forest of Dean than the M25.

We continued at high speed weaving in and out of the traffic, sometimes in the oncoming lane and sometimes on the hard shoulder. Unfortunately the hard shoulder was merely a track along the adjoining field. The mud was such that the windscreen wipers could not cope and the driver was driving with his head out of the window. From time to time, Primakov's assistant turned around to me riding in the back and said, "Half-past-two." I gathered that this was the time scheduled for lunch. Whilst I was convinced that we would have an accident, I tried to pretend to be perfectly at ease. In fact I was praying hard that if we did have an accident that I should be killed rather than maimed. The idea of lying seriously injured in a Soviet hospital seemed far worse than sudden death.

We eventually arrived at a heavily guarded establishment that turned out to be one of the KGB's principal bases, roughly equivalent to that of the CIA at Fort Langley near Washington. We had a very enjoyable, useful and interesting lunch there without touching on any sensitive issues of intelligence. When I had returned to London, I debriefed to the appropriate authorities.

"I think," I said, "that I was probably the first English person to have been inside that particular establishment."
My colleague replied, "I think not. There may have been three before you, Burgess, McLean and Philby."
"Well then, I was the first non-professional to have been there!"

The level of chaos in Moscow at this time is illustrated by the following extracts from a private note that I sent to the FCO following my November 1991 visit to Moscow:

> "The state of chaos throughout the former Soviet Union is increasing. The decision-making process is almost paralysed. Where decisions are made there seems little way of implementing them. The 'machine of government' has all but collapsed.
>
> In the field of defence, Marshal Shaposhnikov and General Lobov appear unable or unwilling to face realities and make decisions. There is still much concern over the custody, ownership and safety of nuclear weapons in the Ukraine and Kazakhstan. Yesterday Shaposhnikov was told by the General Staff that there was no money available to pay the armed forces in December. Some officers are now being paid less than bus drivers."

A year later in May 1992, I found myself involved in a highly unusual task together with Admiral Bill Crowe, a former chairman of the US Joint Chiefs-of-Staff. We were supported by Alton Frye, a Director of the US Council on Foreign Relations, and Ernst van Eeghen, Joint Secretary of the De Burght Conferences and well known in the Soviet Union. The De Burght Conferences, initiated in January 1988, were principally concerned with human rights, religious, economic and financial issues between the West and the former Soviet Union.

The issue with which we were principally concerned was the division of the Soviet Black Sea Fleet between Russia, Ukraine and the CIS. On arrival in Kiev we were warmly greeted and had meetings with President Leonid Kravchuk, the Deputy Ukrainian Foreign Minister, General Morozov, the Minister of Defence, and various senior officials. The Ukrainian position was that part of the Soviet Black Sea Fleet now belonged to the Ukraine. The fleet consisted of over three hundred naval and auxiliary units and was based at Sebastopol, now a Ukrainian territory. It was not entirely clear why they wanted it or what they thought they could do with it. Nevertheless, it was theirs. The Russian position was that this was a strategic force and, in the CIS agreement, strategic forces continued to belong to Russia. It rapidly became clear to Bill

Crowe and I that this was a political issue which had little to do with military capability. Although we were not permitted to go to Sebastopol to visit the fleet, it was fairly obvious that its military capability was now extremely limited and as one person described it was not much more than a "rust bucket".

During our visit we were taken to visit a Ukrainian factory which had for many years been making small, lightweight parts for the Soviet arms industry. There was now no call for it. The management had decided to transfer its output from the military to the civilian sector by producing medical equipment. The enterprise in its heyday had employed some ten thousand people. This workforce had already been reduced by half. The half that remained was now idle because they were unable to get the raw material, aluminium, from Russia. Our Dutch colleague, a born entrepreneur, told the plant manager that he could arrange a contract to supply his factory with all the aluminium that he needed at a price that could not be matched anywhere in the world. There followed an extraordinary conversation with the 'deaf'. It was clear that the plant manager had no idea what a contract meant nor who might sign it on behalf of the enterprise. In Soviet days they just placed an order and the raw materials arrived. The fracture between western and eastern economies could not have been more starkly illustrated.

We were well supported by the British Chargé d'Affaires who was working from several rooms in a local Kiev hotel - the Americans had managed to afford a suitable property for an embassy and were represented by an ambassador. Our chargé kindly gave a reception for Bill Crowe and I together with high-level Ukrainian officials to mark a very successful visit. The British embassy in Moscow had sent a young assistant naval attaché to Kiev to help in the office. Talking with Admiral Crowe, who had described to him how well we had been received at a high level in Kiev on a matter which we considered to be of international importance, he added his own comment, "Oh yes sir. These people here will talk to absolutely anybody."

During our time in Kiev it had become clear that an issue of considerably greater importance than the Black Sea Fleet was that of the control of the formerly Soviet ballistic missiles based in Ukraine – a subject which occupied the majority of our time when we went on to Moscow. During that visit Bill Crowe took the opportunity to visit the widow of former Soviet Marshal Ogarkov whom I myself had met in London. During the 1980s Ogarkov had been hosted by Bill Crowe on an official visit to the United States. Ogarkov, who was accompanied by his wife, was shown around personally by Bill and saw every aspect of the vast array of weaponry that was available to the US President. At the personal level, they got on extremely well and as a result a return visit was arranged.

I found Bill Crowe's descriptions of both these visits extraordinarily interesting. In Russia he was shown the scenes of the great battles of World War II. Bill told me that he had never appreciated the scale of the fighting on the Eastern Front. He said to me that the Russians were moving around armies in much the same way as the Americans would have moved divisions. During their visit to Stalingrad, Ogarkov had said that the real heroes of the Battle of Stalingrad were not the Russian soldiers but those of Germany. The Russians were defending their own homes. The Germans were operating in hostile territory and were taking appalling casualties.

Ogarkov was known as a 'Gorbachev man'. When the Yeltsin coup occurred it was reported that Ogarkov had committed suicide by hanging. There was at that time some doubt as to the veracity of this report. Ogarkov was certainly dead but that he should have hanged himself seemed entirely out of character to all who knew him. All Soviet officers carried their own pistols and there was much comment on the proposition that if Ogarkov had to be eliminated it would have been easier to fake realistically his death by hanging than by shooting. Bill had no intention whatsoever of fuelling these rumours. His visit to Ogarkov's widow was a genuine expression of the personal relationship that he, the Chairman of the US Chief-of-Staff, had established with the head of the armed forces of the Soviet Union.

During our time in Moscow, Bill and I had a long meeting with Marshal Shaposhnikov who was then Supreme Commander of the CIS forces. Our discussions focused almost entirely on nuclear issues. It became increasingly apparent that there was some justification for the Russian fears that the Ukrainians could have acquired the ability to fire the armed strategic missiles based in Ukraine without any authority from Moscow. We talked detailed matters of strategic missile control and discovered that the Russians had nothing to compare with the sophisticated PAL (Permissive Action Link) technology fitted in western strategic systems. These matters were undoubtedly of deep strategic importance. As I retired to bed that night, it occurred to me that if some ten years before when I was a NATO Supreme Commander, I had told my staff that within ten years I should be talking in depth with Soviet generals on matters of strategic weapon control, they would have sent for the men in white coats. We later met with the Russian Deputy Minister of Foreign Affairs and the Chairman of the International Affairs Council of the Russian Federation.

Our visit ended with a journey to the north of Moscow to visit Zagorsk, the centre of the Russian Orthodox Church. The devout nature of those who served it and the magnificent beauty of the buildings underlined the extraordinary contradictions between the history and traditions of Mother Russia and the brutal conditions imposed on it by the Communist Party of the Soviet Union.

In our final signed report to President Yeltsin and to President Kravchuk, we attempted to take the heat out of this dispute. We wrote:

> We have been impressed by the commitment of the governments in Kiev and Moscow to pursue a negotiated solution with good will. ...We believe that with the declared goodwill we have found, an equitable solution can be reached. Such a solution will be more easily reached if first consideration is given to identifying and meeting the maritime interests of Russia, Ukraine, Georgia

and the CIS, in the light of inevitable budget reductions, rather than to the simple division of present assets.

Admirals can also be diplomats.

Whilst these formal contacts were being developed with the Soviets, there were also taking place a considerable number of other informal contacts, both personal and collective, with the Soviet Union and the Warsaw Pact states.

On one of my trips to Moscow my visit coincided with October 21st, Trafalgar Day. With my encouragement, the naval attaché had invited Admiral Chernavin, who was head of the Soviet navy, to be guest of honour. He had also, with considerable enterprise, invited the French naval attaché to give the speech in honour of Lord Nelson. At the last moment the French naval attaché himself was unable to attend and passed the task to his assistant, a young lieutenant commander. He was understandably and clearly nervous but made a brilliant speech centred on the question - why was Trafalgar such a great triumph for the British? His response was because the French fought so well. Chernavin obviously thoroughly enjoyed the occasion but was clearly somewhat bewildered by it all.

I had previously paid a courtesy call on Admiral Chernavin at his office as head of the Soviet navy, a call that was kindly arranged for me by Yevgeny Primakov. I was driven to the naval headquarters where I was met by a naval captain and shown to the waiting room of Chernavin's office. I saw that there were some interesting models of what appeared to be underwater vessels but that I neither recognised nor understood. After a short wait, I was shown into his office where he greeted me warmly. I said that I had previously known him as an opponent when I was the NATO Commander, Eastern Atlantic and he was Commander of the Soviet Northern Fleet. But now the Royal Navy was building a new relationship with the Soviet navy. I told him that I had then kept a photograph of him in my office. He immediately responded, "and I have a photo of you on my desk now." It was taken from an international naval journal for which I wrote a monthly editorial. I found Chernavin friendly, personable and not without style.

There was no doubt that the Gorbachev era had also brought with it a new and much improved relationship between our two navies, a relationship whose warmth accelerated in the early 1990s culminating in the celebrations of the first British convoy of war supplies for the Russians which had arrived in Archangel at the end of August 1941. HMS LONDON, flying the flag of the Flag Officer, 1st Flotilla, accompanied by RFA TIDESPRING made a rendezvous at sea with a Russian force of a cruiser and three destroyers. The British naval attaché reported the sight of the two navies entering together the waters of the Northern Fleet base as "One of many emotional moments with which everyone was touched. From then on, the events generated more and more warmth as they proceeded in Murmansk and Archangel." The veterans groups from both sides received great hospitality. In Archangel, LONDON's 'ship open to visitors' was an enormous success.

The naval attaché, who was embarked and made welcome in a Russian Krivak II destroyer for the passage from Murmansk to Archangel, made a chilling report of the state of maintenance of the ship, its austere and sometimes spartan standard of accommodation, the relation of the captain to the Zampolit who acted in all disciplinary matters without any reference to him, the lack of safety procedures and the apparently unstructured nature of the bridge routine whilst at sea. As a former British Flag Officer Sea Training, I found the report almost beyond belief.

My final visit to Moscow in February 1997 was at the personal invitation of Yevgeny Primakov who was then Foreign Minister. My first call was on Andrei Kokoshin, who was now Deputy Minister of Defence. He greeted me very warmly. He was clearly now in a very much improved position vis-à-vis his uniformed colleagues. We spent a considerable time discussing the need for a new overarching framework for European security. It was clear however that the Russians were becoming increasingly frustrated that their own ideas were consistently rejected by the

West in a situation in which they felt encircled by NATO enlargement. They had lost the cold war but still felt threatened by a cold peace. However, a recent visit by the British Secretary of State for Defence had been adjudged very successful. Kokoshin described relations with Britain as being good. It was relations with NATO that were the problem.

I had similar long and purposeful discussions in the Russian Foreign Office with the head of the Planning Staff. He outlined proposals on military measures and political and economic principles which in my view amounted to a new 'European Agenda'. Not all would be welcomed by the West but I found it encouraging in seeming to offer a new path away from the military orientated exchanges on NATO enlargement towards a longer term more balanced agreement on the future European political, economic and security relationship.

I also had long and most cordial talks at IMEMO with Mr Martinov, now the director, and a number of former colleagues of Mr Primakov. The thrust of our discussions was aimed at increasing the degree of 'track two' (non governmental – institute-to-institute) contacts over a wide range of issues, including the measures necessary to avoid the dangers of escalating social and ethnic tensions in some eastern European countries. We also addressed the possibility of Russia taking a somewhat higher profile position in the security discussions of the northeast Asian region. There was no lack of goodwill in this direction on both sides but the financing of such a regular track two dialogue presented clear constraints. On the following day, I had similar and constructive discussions in the Institute of Europe.

I completed this visit, accepting a most welcome offer of a visit to Leningrad. I travelled there overnight by train. The compartments held four bunk beds clearly allocated without attention to age, sex or infirmity. At the end of the carriage corridor there was a large samovar heated by an open fire. Fortunately we had imbibed considerable quantities of vodka before we embarked. The undoubted hazards of the journey rather passed me by. Despite the typical run-down nature of the city, one could not help but be struck by the magnificence of its buildings, many of them restored after the terrible siege of the city by the Germans in World War II. The Hermitage Museum was breathtaking in the depth and breadth of its collections. I had had no idea that it held the finest collection of French impressionist paintings anywhere in the world.

At Pavlov's Palace, the Hall of Mirrors was overwhelming in its beauty. I was well aware of the Painted Hall at Greenwich, well known as Europe's finest hall – but the competition must have been a very close run thing. The theatre, the part played by Leningrad (then Petrograd) in the Russian Revolution,and the horrific conditions of the World War II siege, all helped to provide a picture of Russia's history so inwardly and outwardly different to the face presented by Soviet Communism. Nevertheless, on my return to London, I wrote a somewhat pessimistic report:

> My overall conclusion is that the internal situation In Russia is seriously in danger of complete breakdown. Public patience in acquiescing to the present lack of order is almost certainly limited. How limited, only time will tell. If the present difficulties can be overcome, then the longer-term outlook appears more reassuring. But in the interim, Western approaches will need to be handled with greater sensitivity than is as indicated by the mess we have, regrettably, got ourselves into over NATO enlargementI believe that the breakdown did not occur reflects credit on Yevgeny Primakov's short tenure as Prime Minister, during which he achieved successfully a number of very difficult reforms. This very success may well have contributed to his removal from power by President Yeltsin only a year later. Primakov's subsequent bid in the Dumas for the Presidency was overtaken by that of President Vladimir Putin, to whom Primakov later became a political ally and adviser.

The transition from Communism towards modern democratic government inspired deep emotions amongst very many of the Russian people. They were leaving a domain that they understood, even if they had not liked, for an unknown future. I remember asking two senior academics in Moscow what they meant by democracy. The first replied, "Anti communism," – the second, "Not winning every election by a hundred and twenty percent of the votes." For many the heart was being torn out of the Soviet Union, which was now without the power to influence or to lead a new Commonwealth of Independent States.

Today, amongst very large sections of the Russian population, Gorbachev is highly unpopular. It is said that he destroyed a system but put nothing in its place. Although I personally still admire Gorbachev, I believe there is much to be said for this view. Kruschev's period in office is perhaps best summarised in the reported exchange between himself and the United States President in the Oval Office at the White House:

"Welcome to America, Mr Chairman. In a word, how are things today in your great country?"
"Mr President, Good."
"And in more than one word?"
"Not very good."

Now, largely on account of American policy and actions in the Middle East, the fulfilment of a lasting constructive relationship with Russia within a wider Europe must remain a dream.

Chapter 7

Argentina and the Falkland Islands

"In war all is simple, but the simple is still very difficult."
                                                                Clausewitz

In my interview for the chairmanship of the Royal Institute I had made it clear that a role that I thought the Institute should perform would be to be able to speak to foreign countries authoritatively when the relationship between the governments made such inter-governmental communication inappropriate. Having been directly involved with the Falkland Islands' war, I was much concerned that there were apparently very few efforts being made to re-establish a relationship between Britain and Argentina. The two governments remained at loggerheads on all issues. I was aware that the Königswinter conferences, which had successfully helped to restore relations between Britain and Germany after World War II had been initiated only four years after World War II had ended. I therefore set about trying to re-establish some institute-to-institute relationship between Chatham House and Argentina. My problem was twofold and linked. I needed to find funding and I needed to find an appropriate institute in Argentina.

Bearing in mind, that Chatham House was politically neutral in Britain, most institutes of international affairs in other countries were closely linked to a particular political regime. The Ford Foundation in America was well disposed to my requests for funding but needed to be convinced that my partner institute in Buenos Aires was politically respectable. To identify such was not easy and took nearly two years. The institute that we finally identified was the Centro de Investigaciones Europeo-Latinoamericanas (EURAL). The director, Atilio Borón, was extremely helpful in making arrangements for me to visit Buenos Aires – although it took some considerable time to achieve. One essential step in the process of reconciliation was the arrangement of a small meeting with several members of the Argentine Senate – mostly elderly and dyed-in-the-wool socialista. Since some of the Argentines were unwilling to travel to Britain and we were not at that time able to travel to Argentina, the meeting took place in March 1985, clandestinely and on neutral ground in Germany, under the auspices of the German Institute, the DGAP.

The meeting was very formal but we did make progress in trying to establish further relationships. At this time the Parliamentary Joint British-Argentine Committee were also trying to re-establish communication and had had one successful meeting in Canada. This and other links between Buenos Aires and London successfully broke the ice in helping to clarify some of the immediate issues. The parliamentarians had however run into difficulty in arranging a further meeting. In Argentina they were in contact with Carlos Munis, a former ambassador to the United Nations who was now President of the Council for Argentine International Relations (CARI). The Argentine side kept on making difficulties over the agenda, apparently as excuses for delay. The British side took the view that it did not matter what the agenda would be – it would be helpful just to meet and talk. I was asked to see if, during my planned visit, I could help break this logjam.

My visit to Buenos Aires eventually took place in July 1989, there having been a last minute delay to avoid the political situation resulting from the change of government from President Alfonsín of the Radicale party to that of the Peronista with Carlos Menem of the Justicialist party as President. I landed at Buenos Aires mid-morning to find that my first engagement was the same afternoon. On the journey from the airport I was struck by the extent of poverty that was revealed by the large areas of shack-like dwellings that surrounded the striking architecture of the city. My first meeting, the arrangements for which had been made by Atilio Borón, was with the newly appointed Argentine Foreign Minister, Domingo Cavallo[9] who was supported by a team of his Foreign Office officials. I explained that the object of my visit was

---

[9] *He was by profession an economist and later became a special advisor in Moscow on matters of economic transformation.*

to seek an informal channel of communication between our two countries since realism dictated that there was little chance of any early and meaningful government-to-government relationship. Without some channel for the exchange of ideas between the two countries, the British-Argentine relationship was unlikely to improve. I also mentioned the task that I had been set by the British Parliamentary Group which had asked me to discuss the situation with the head of a major institute in Buenos Aires, the Council for International Relations (CARI). I said I was very disappointed to discover on my arrival that Ambassador Munis was not in Buenos Aires. To my surprise and delight the Foreign Minister replied, "Well, that's very interesting because I'm having a drink with him tonight." A minion was despatched from the meeting who then came back some twenty minutes later and delivered the message that a meeting had been arranged for me with Munis at his institute at nine o'clock the following morning.

When I arrived at CARI next day, I was well received by Ambassador Munis, who spoke excellent English. We had a brief introductory discussion and I explained that my mission on behalf of the British side of the British-Argentine Parliamentary Group was to see if we could move towards a date for their next meeting. Our parliamentarians had become somewhat discouraged by what appeared to be delaying tactics on the Argentine side. Munis explained that they could not commit themselves to a further meeting with the British side without the support of the Argentine government. I responded, "My dear ambassador, yesterday afternoon I was in a long meeting with the Foreign Minister of your new government, Domingo Cavallo, and he assured me on no less than three occasions that the project for a further meeting between parliamentarians had his full support. You do have the support of the government." Munis looked very embarrassed. He had been supporting the previous Radicale government for so long that he had forgotten that he was no longer part of the government. He was left with no leg to stand on and my mission got off to a good start.

Returning to the meeting with Domingo Cavallo - I was surprised and delighted at the constructive nature of our discussion. He also told me that the previous president, President Alfonsín, had just returned to Buenos Aires for the first time since his recent ousting and suggested that I meet with him. I agreed because I was anxious to sample as wide a range of opinions in Buenos Aires as was possible during my short visit. The visit was arranged for me and a car organised to take me to the villa where he was now staying. I was warned that the situation internally in Argentina was still very sensitive and that the villa might well be surrounded by a crowd. I was told that, on passing through the crowd, I was on no account to say a single word of English. During the journey there I had considerable thoughts about what I would say if someone stamped accidentally on my foot whilst I was trying to reach the door - without coming to any conclusion. Fortunately there was no great crowd and I was ushered in without ceremony.

This was one of the most difficult meetings that I remember. Alfonsín spoke no English and I had no Spanish. I sat on a sofa to his right whilst the interpreter was on the other side of a quite large room. The interpreter spoke fairly clearly but was not very loud. Being rather deaf in my right ear, I had to turn my head to the right to hear the interpreter – which meant that I could not retain eye contact with Alfonsin. Sadly I failed to record immediately afterwards the outline of our discussion – but it was clear to me that what he had to say amounted to little more than a political apologia for what had been done in initiating the war. I do recall him saying that it was the military Junta that made the decision in late 1981 to invade and to make the preliminary military preparations. This was not known by the highest political authorities until the following year, when the momentum of events made it impossible for the government to draw back - their confidence in success being bolstered by the British Government's announced decision to withdraw the South Atlantic guard ship, HMS ENDURANCE.

I returned to London somewhat encouraged by my visit and particularly with the very useful contact I had made with EURAL. My general impression was that there was greater flexibility in Buenos Aires with regard to the future British-Argentine relationship than I would find in London. My debrief with the Foreign Office did not discourage me from this view. Nevertheless, for reasons that I did not understand, but were probably related to the change of government in Argentina, Margaret Thatcher drew back a little from her previous confrontational attitude towards Buenos Aires.

There followed several years of informal exchanges dealing with every aspect of the British-Argentine relationship – from sovereignty of the Falkland Islands, to the local relationship between the islanders and the Argentine mainland, fish, oil, communications and culture. At the government level, there was a gradual but welcome improvement in the government-to-government relationship. In 1989 agreement was reached between the two governments to hold talks aimed at restoring full diplomatic relations between the two countries. The talks were held in Madrid in two sessions about six months apart. On our side, Ambassador Sir Crispin Tickell, who had been our ambassador to the United Nations and was a close advisor to Margaret Thatcher on environmental matters, conducted the talks. On the Argentine side was Garcia del Solar, the former head of the Foreign Ministry in Buenos Aires, whom I had got to know following my first visit. The talks, following the second session, were successfully concluded, an exchange of ambassadors being agreed. Formal diplomatic relations were restored in 1990.

Not long after, I happened to meet Crispin Tickell. I offered him my congratulations and asked him if he would, on the next occasion that he met his Argentine 'co-negotiator', also give him my congratulations. He said he would be delighted to do so. He told me that Garcia del Solar had sent his kind regards to me. He also said that he knew that when Admiral Jim Eberle first came to Buenos Aires, although he had said otherwise, he was in fact a representative of the Foreign Office and the British Government. Crispin explained that this was definitely not so and that I was acting in an entirely independent capacity. He had not been able to convince Garcia of this.

This represented a problem I had met before. Because Chatham House was the Royal Institute, its position as being entirely independent of the government, whilst in close contact with the British Foreign Office, was not easily understood. The Foreign Office was very sensitive to this because I sometimes expressed views that were not in line with the official Government position. On one occasion the Permanent Secretary of the Foreign Office summoned me to express his concern at the tone of some of my discussions with my Russian colleagues. I assured him that, on every relevant occasion, I always tried to make clear that my views were my own and did not necessarily reflect those of the British Government. He did not seem entirely convinced. However, I assured him that I had made similar noises on my first and subsequent visits to Argentina.

At the non-governmental level, our discussions led to the formation of an Argentine-British Conference, a number of exchange visits, and a general expression of good will. The first meetings of the unofficial Argentine–British Conference took place at Streatley-on-Thames in April 1990 with the object of encouraging understanding and contact between the two countries, and providing an unofficial but influential forum for the exchange of views and ideas of mutual interest. It was chaired by Viscount Montgomery of Alamein. It was undoubtedly a success, not least in providing an opportunity for a wide ranging exchange of views from both sides. We agreed to meet again in a year's time in Argentina. This took place in the southern part of the country at Baraloche, a delightful, wild and beautiful part of Patagonia. It provided a splendid backdrop for our discussions - but I seem to remember that it had a greater effect on the tone of our discussions rather than their content or outcome. There was no disguising the fundamental Argentine belief that the sovereignty of the Falkland Islands belonged to them. The degree of diplomacy required was great and I often found myself in at the deep end. But at least we all enjoyed ourselves.

Following the meeting, I was invited by Governor Jose Bordon of Mendoza Province, which lies in the east of the country in the shadow of the Andes Mountains, to be his guest there. He was in the early stages of considering his future candidacy for President as an eventual successor to Carlos Menem. I was most warmly received by the Governor, and found the country there, and its wine, quite delightful. However, I found it a trifle 'chilling' when my host told me that he, the Governor, had had to seek the approval of the local military commander in his province, an army general, before issuing an invitation for me to come to Mendoza as his personal guest.

The third meeting in Cambridge in September 1992 was marked by it being the first occasion when representatives of the Falkland Island Government and the British Foreign Office attended. The meeting also benefited by a wide-ranging and influential non-governmental attendance on both sides. During the course of those few days an incident occurred, the nature of which I cannot remember, which nearly caused a walkout of the Argentine side. We were fortunately able just to avoid this. Our meeting was not without problems, however. One of the Falkland Island Legislature's representatives was a former chief of police of the islands, Terry Burns. He was a delightful man, but was not familiar with the niceties of international politics. A particular matter relating to the future of the islands was the clear distinction to be drawn between "the wishes of the islanders" and the "interests of the islanders". The Foreign Office was studiously careful never to mention the expression "the wishes of the islanders" because these could not be controlled by London. It was therefore very important to the FCO that we should only use the term "the best interests of the islanders", because this could be deemed to be determined in London. The chief of police, not being aware of this nuance, used either term, whichever occurred to him at the time. I took particular delight at such moments in watching the expressions of horror on the faces of my Foreign Office colleagues when he got it wrong.

During the 1990s, the Argentine–British Conference continued successfully to provide a channel for progressing the Argentine-British relationship. The agenda covered every aspect of this relationship bar the issue of sovereignty – although the Argentinians from time to time tried obliquely to put this back on the agenda. Economic issues were always high on the agenda. Fishing rights within the waters surrounding the Falkland Islands' waters were a constant matter for disagreement, with the reported decline of certain species being a particular issue. Seismic research in the vicinity of the islands, and nearer to the Argentine coastline, had suggested the presence of large quantities of oil. This was clearly a potential issue, either for dispute or co-operation. My own view, which I had expressed strongly, was that if commercial quantities of oil were to be exploited, it was highly unlikely that the oil companies would be willing to establish terminal facilities, such as refining, both on the islands and on the mainland. In due course therefore a negotiated agreement would be essential before exploitation could be effective.

We have now reached the twenty-fifth anniversary of the Argentine invasion. A visit by Her Majesty The Queen and the Duke of Edinburgh to the islands for this occasion has taken place. Almost inevitably this will provide new political pressures in Argentina for a resolution of the sovereignty issue. However, the last ten years of the government-to-government relationship had been largely sterile and there has been little or no progress in a solution to the fundamental problem of sovereignty of the Islands. In the years following the resumption of diplomatic relations, Guido Di Tella offered, at an appropriate level, some hope of a measured approach to the problem of sovereignty for the Falklands Islands. Since his death there seems to be nobody in Argentina willing to follow his example.

In 2001, Argentina suffered severe economic problems, which led to the resignation of President, De La Rua. His successor,

President Nestor Kirchner has not shown any interest in the resolution of the Falklands problem.

Within the region, the economic intergovernmental organisation of Mercosur has had little impact on the health of the Latin American economies in general. Strong socialist governments hold sway in the north of the continent whilst elections including that of the presidency are due to take place in Argentina in 2007. There is no evidence to suggest that there might be any early fundamental change in the present Argentine government climate. Within the Islands, the economic situation is basically good, with the fishing licensing system working well and providing both revenue and measures of conservation. Recent exploration in the surrounding waters has produced further encouraging evidence of oil and mineral resources. The scene is therefore set for a continuing lack of any progress in the political field which might lead to a solution of the sovereignty issue. However, since 1990, there have been a number of international peacekeeping and peace enforcement operations in which the armed forces of both sides have been jointly involved, sometimes under British command and sometimes under Argentine military command. Bilateral military contacts have also been established on an annual basis, resulting in some Argentine officers undergoing training in Britain and British officers in Argentina. There is a programme for an exchange of high level visits. This is encouraging in the longer term and needs to be quietly nurtured.

Could there be another military-led attempt at a solution? Regrettably, I detect a somewhat complacent view among some in saying that a repeat invasion could not be successful, because there is now an international-sized airport at Mount Pleasant which would permit rapid British re-enforcement of the Islands; an option not previously available. Runways, like aircraft carriers, can however be 'taken out'. What is surely required is an agreed political programme of confidence-building political and economic measures aimed at a long-term compromise acceptable to Britain, Argentina and the Islanders. At the moment, we only hear the sound of one hand clapping.

Chapter 8

The Asia Pacific Region

"If you come to a fork in the road, take it."

Yogi Bear

My personal experience as a young man in the Far East provided a good basis for me to help direct more of the Institute's research work towards the Asian region. Our Asian programme, under the very able direction of Dr Brian Bridges, a fluent Japanese linguist, sprang quickly into action. My first overseas visit to Japan on behalf of the Institute was in April 1984. On arrival in Tokyo I found myself initially in the firm hands of the International Bureau of the Japanese Liberal Democratic Party (LDP) which then formed the Japanese Government. My programme included addressing some seventy party activists and LDP Diet members and press interviews. This was heady stuff of a party political nature with which I was not entirely at ease.

However, my programme soon came under the proper guidance of the British embassy, with appropriate calls being arranged for me, accompanied by Brian Bridges. These included to the Foreign Office (Gaimusho); to the Ministry of Trade and Industry (MITI), which was the power-house of the Japanese industrial economy; and to the Keidanren, the Japanese equivalent of the Confederation of British Industry (CBI). The Keidanren's role, power and influence were far greater than that of the CBI however. I found these visits very formal, but also sufficiently interesting to allow me to relax – which I did - only to be told very quietly and properly by Dr Bridges that in Japan it was not polite to appear relaxed when dealing with high government officials. There was much, despite my post-war experiences, that I still needed to learn about Japan and its culture.

Later, I was talking to a young British businessman in Japan who described to me an incident that had brought home to him the deep cultural differences that divide our two nations. His

Japanese office colleague who had much enjoyed a short holiday in Europe, during which he had visited London, now wished to return for a longer visit to England. "Tell me," he said, "about the mores of the English social character. What, for instance, are the things that the English do not like to talk about?" After some considerable thought, for this was very much a Japanese rather than a British question, he replied, "Well, one thing that the English don't like talking about is death." "That's very strange," responded his Japanese colleague, "because I know that you get married in graveyards." Our nations have a lot to learn about each other.

I also paid a call at the Japanese Centre for International Affairs (JCIE). This was led by Tadashi Yamamoto, a man of remarkably wide international experience who had close contacts at the high political levels throughout Japan, and who was held in very high regard by the Japanese bureaucracy. For some fifteen years we worked together very happily in the closest co-operation. He held my total respect.

When I returned to London, I found the staff at Chatham House returning to normal after the events of a week-long police siege of St James's Square following the death of police constable Yvonne Fletcher, who was shot dead in the street from the windows of the nearby Libyan embassy during a peaceful demonstration.

Following my visit to Tokyo, I was determined to further strengthen our East Asia Programme and to enhance our close relations with the JCIE. I also strongly encouraged the efforts of William Wallace, my deputy, in supporting the efforts in London to promote a new non-governmental group aimed at strengthening Anglo-Japanese relations.

The flowering of Anglo-Japanese relations had begun in the early 1980's, when a new sense of globalisation was born, against whose background governments sought further to broaden and strengthen their bilateral relationships. At this time, a number of British luminaries such as Sir Julian Ridsdale, a former pre-World War II ambassador in Tokyo, began encouraging younger members of the House of Commons to visit Japan. Amongst these was Richard Needham, a prominent Conservative member of parliament who had had experience of the very successful Anglo-German Königswinter conferences. In London, he met Yukio Satoh who had been sent by the Japanese government to seek possibilities for founding a Japan-UK 'wise men's group'.

In the summer of 1983, Richard Needham, with the assistance of a fellow Conservative member of parliament, Richard Forman, began assembling names of those who might support an initiative to form such a non-governmental Anglo-Japanese group to act in a similar role to that of Königswinter. Sir James Prior, then a member of Mrs Thatcher's government and later to become deputy chairman of GEC, agreed to lead the group. The idea attracted a number of other influential names, including Sir Michael Wilford, a former ambassador in Tokyo, Sir Peter Parker, Chris Patten and a number of the captains of the city and of British industry. The necessary funding and charitable status were achieved. It was named the UK-Japan 2000 Group.

Following a successful visit by the Japanese Prime Minister to London in the summer of 1984, Mrs Thatcher lent her weight to the project, appreciating the role that Japan could play in strengthening Britain's industrial base and bringing fresh ideas and disciplines to the workplace. From Japan's point of view, she much needed a bridgehead for commercial expansion into the European Common Market. At the UK government level, the Foreign Office and Department of Trade and Industry were increasingly recognising, not only the important part that Japan was playing in the markets of Southeast Asia, but also in its investments in British industry.

In 1994 the former Vice-Minister for Foreign Affairs in Japan, Hisashi Owada, had described the UK-Japan government relationship as "...in excellent shape, reminiscent of the days of the Anglo-Japanese alliance at the turn of the century. I believe that our two nations are called upon to bring in a new era of Anglo-Japanese alliance, building a new partnership." The UK-

Japan 2000 Group was set up to help to give substance to this goal.

The founding prospectus of the group expressed its role and purpose as: "At all levels, relations between Japan and the United Kingdom are cordial but not close. The depth of personal contact and mutual understanding enjoyed by Britain in her relations with other major partners does not match good relations between the two governments. There are clearly historical, geographical and cultural reasons for this. The first objective of the 2000 Group will therefore be to promote contact between the two societies in general, and in particular, prominent figures in all areas of public life."

In early 1985 Margaret Thatcher wrote to the Japanese Prime Minister, Yasuhiro Nakasone, seeking to improve our bilateral relations by "examining the scope for practical co-operation between our two countries much more closely." She received a welcoming response from Japan expressing "our common belief in the values of freedom, democracy and the free market economy." By the spring, the scene was set for the first visit of the UK-Japan 2000 Group to Japan under the chairmanship of Lord Prior, with Chatham House having undertaken the task of administrative support.

In preparation for the imminent departure of the group for Tokyo, members of the group gathered in the private room of the Prime Minister in the House of Commons. I well remember that I had been asked to open the meeting with a short account of the group's role and purpose. Describing this meeting subsequently to a senior political friend, I said that I had hardly spoken for more than one or two minutes before Margaret Thatcher took over. "You were able to speak for a whole two minutes," he responded, "You did well!"

During this meeting the Prime Minister expressed her full support and handed over a warm personal letter for us to deliver personally to Prime Minister Nakasone. As a very productive meeting drew to a close, Jim Prior raised the matter of a suitable 'presento' for us to give to Nakasone-san, of a quality that such an important occasion called for, and that was within the group's means to afford, the Foreign Office having declined to help. Mrs Thatcher then set off 'in full flight', emphasising that what we were to take should not only represent the undeniable skills of the British in scientific research but also in our abilities in the field of industrial and technical manufacture. She went on for some time. Eventually Jim Prior, who was no particular friend of the British Prime Minister, interrupted with a light-hearted response, "Perhaps then Prime Minister, we should take a nuclear power station." Mrs Thatcher was not amused. As we left the room, the temperature was a good deal lower than when we had arrived. Nevertheless, the group retained her firm personal support.

We eventually settled on the presentation of a rather nice early painting of Whitehall Palace in Westminster. This we delivered to Prime Minister Nakasone in the Japanese parliament building when we made our call there on arrival in Tokyo. His reception was extremely welcoming but he apologised that he could only spend a short time talking with us since he had to go to a session of the Diet so as to answer questions from Diet members. "This is a problem," he said with a broad smile, "that we have inherited from your parliamentary democracy." The group continued the practice of a meeting with Prime Minister of the host country prior to each of its meetings.

At the early meetings of the group, we had to overcome an atmosphere of traditional reserve on the Japanese side and a tendency of the British to do too much of the talking. However, as experience was gained by both sides during the annual conferences that followed, and under the skilful guidance of its two chairmen, the group developed its own dynamics. At the personal level, our meetings provided a most valuable forum for strengthening the UK-Japan relationship. In those early days, the thrust of our discussions usually centred on the British desire better to understand the enormous international success of the Japanese economy. The Japanese side sought to gain from British experience in the wider field of international security and diplomacy. Later, as the Japanese internal economy began to falter, and the success of Mrs Thatcher's policies on industrial and financial deregulation became evident, it was the Japanese, rather than the British who became the 'demandeur' – "How did the City of London achieve the 'Big Bang'?"

The group benefited greatly from the personal participation, under the skilful chairmanship of their chairman, Motoo Shiina, of some fifteen top level Japanese participants. These included distinguished industrialists, such as Dr Akio Morita, the legendry head of Sony who coined the expression 'glocalisation', Dr Shoichiro Toyoda, head of the Toyota car manufacturer, and Dr Tadahiro Sekimoto, head of NEC. The political and academic community were represented by similarly distinguished figures such as Japanese Professor Atsushi Shimokobe and Ambassador Tadao Kato. The British representation was similarly well matched. In 1987, Lord Patrick Jenkin took over the chairmanship of the British group, to be followed in 1991 by Lord David Howell.

During the fifteen years in which Tadashi Yamamoto and I acted as joint secretaries to the 2000 Group, and often as rapporteurs of the group's meetings, the agenda ranged over a very wide range of bilateral and global subjects, economic, cultural, social, educational, scientific, technological, business, education, urban, and political-security issues. In the interval between the annual meetings, there was a great deal of contact, centred in London on Chatham House and in Tokyo on the Japan Centre for International Exchange, to progress the outcome of each meeting and to prepare the ground for the next. But the group was not only a talk shop. As the cohesion of the group continued to grow, it spawned a new enthusiasm for a wide range of outside activities, large and small.

The two very successful major events, the 1991 Japan Festival in the UK and the 1998 British Festival in Japan, each centring on the people-to-people relationship, were landmarks in UK Japan co-operation. The visiting Japanese research fellows' programme at Chatham House was also very successfully expanded, with much mutual benefit. There was increased interest in Japanese language training, an area in which Sir Peter Parker made a very important contribution; and in the area of teacher exchange (JET). Exchange activities between NGO leaders from the UK and Japan, encouraged and endorsed by the 2000 Group, provided a model for new kinds of collaborative programmes, including the Anglo-Japan High Technology Forum under the UK leadership of Mr Louis Turner. The group lobbied hard and successfully to improve conditions for the exchange of working holidays as a means of enhancing mutual understanding among the youth of both countries.

In early 1992, I received at Chatham House a proposal from Dr Eric Albone, the founding Director of the Clifton Scientific Trust. It was to establish a new Anglo-Japan project. This aimed to develop a partnership in science teaching in schools. Its focus was to help promote creativity in young people in both countries through their participation in open-ended scientific and technological exploration. This promised to strengthen both shared cultural and educational bonds. The development of this proposal received a warm welcome form many directions, both in Japan and Britain. These included not only the two embassies but also the Japan Foundation, the Royal Society, the Daiwa Anglo-Japanese Foundation and the Sasekawa Foundation; also the city of Okayama which had developed links with Bristol. Within the UK-Japan 2000 Group, Lord Jenkin played a lead supporting role.

The first event, a workshop for sharing experiences between science educators from Japan and Britain, was held at Clifton College, Bristol in August 1994. The programme included visits to Bristol University, to Britain's science centre in Cardiff and to Taunton School, where pupils were actively involved in a radio telescope project. The Japanese team included three science teachers from the Musashi High School in Tokyo. As a result, a number of contacts at school level were maintained and progressed which, as the millennium approached, prompted the development of a wider programme of UK-Japan Young Scientist

Partnership workshops. These were aimed at enabling pupils from both countries to experience together the experience of science as a real life challenge.

The first such more ambitious workshop took place in 2001 at the University of Bristol, based on its earth sciences programme. Small UK-Japanese teams of young people from schools across Britain and Japan worked together on ten different projects, one of which focussed on possible origins of the volcanoes on Mars. Subsequently NASA, with whom the students were in daily touch by video conferencing, wrote, "We witnessed real world science education at its finest, and were amazed at the students' initiative and hard work. It demonstrates that, having been given an exciting challenge and necessary resources, young people will far exceed everyone's expectations." One student wrote, "At school I was learning science without being able to apply it; now I know what real science is like...I love it. I have learned loads, not just about science but an awareness of the world."

A second very successful workshop was held in 2004 at the Ritsumeikan University, Kyoto, the results of which were shown in two programmes on Japanese national television. A further such workshop, was held two years later at the University of Surrey that attracted very favourable comment from senior scientists and from the CBI.

Such a bilateral project, when taken in relation to the enormous compass of international relations, may seem somewhat insignificant. However, when seen in the context of the unsatisfactory present state of the British and Japanese educational systems (the British system is almost chaotic – the Japanese system is too rigid) and the increasing role of science in countering global problems such as climate change, the project should be seen as one of high relevance and value for the future. I am reminded that large oak trees grow from small acorns. The continuation and growth of this Anglo-Japanese project from its initiation more than fifteen years before, has been largely due to the persistence and initiative of Dr Eric Albone. Nevertheless, further progress has been slow, due to funding constraints.

During the later years of the century, the UK 2000 Group's agenda further expanded in to the field of the development of civil societies in developing countries. Reflecting its continuing role, the name of the group was also changed to UK-Japan 21st Century Group and brought under the UK administrative responsibility of Asia House in London.

The growing North Korean problems had earlier ensured that it was neither practical nor possible to consider our bilateral relationship with Japan outside the wider context of relationships in northeast Asia, China, Korea, Russia and the United States. This provided the incentive for the formation at Chatham House of an Anglo-South Korean project, centred on industrial issues, which was led by our resident entrepreneur, Louis Turner.

Following the relinquishment of the remnants of post World War II British sovereignty in South East Asia, there had been impressive growth in the concept and cohesion of the Association of South East Asian Nations (ASEAN) and the ASEAN Regional Forum (ARF), despite the formation of other groupings such as the Association of Pacific Economic Communities (APEC) spawned by the United States. In the security field, the Council for Security Co-operation in the Asia Pacific Region (CSCAP), a non-governmental body reporting to the ARF, held regular meetings and conferences in Kuala Lumpur in which Australia played an important part. Britain's formal involvement had been established by the Five Power Agreement of Britain, Australia, Singapore, Malaysia and New Zealand, which had been born at the time of British military withdrawal from Singapore. Britain also retained security responsibilities in Hong Kong. I therefore attended CSCAP meetings, usually held in Kuala Lumpur, wearing my British 'hat', although I maintained an informal European interest in matters of wider and active international concern, such as piracy in the Malacca Straits.

During the 1990's, a particular security issue concerned the South China Sea where China was claiming sovereignty over various islands, the Spratleys and the Paracels. They are also subject to sovereignty and other lesser claims by Taiwan,

Asian Conferences

That's quite enough!

Malaysia, the Philippines, Brunei, and Vietnam. These islands are uninhabited, although fishermen do land from time to time since the local fishing grounds are very productive. They also have potential value in that they may hold sub-surface oil and mineral resources. At a time when the US was preparing to leave their last big base in South East Asia, at Subic Bay in the Philippines, the apparent territorial expansion of China's military influence in the South China Sea became a matter of concern to the members of ASEAN. There was at this stage little evident contact between the countries of South East Asia and those of North East Asia. In between, the serious problems between Taiwan and China formed another major area of potential conflict.

In May 1991 I was invited to speak under the title, "European Perspectives on Security in the Post-Cold War Era" at the twenty-sixth conference of the New Zealand Foreign Policy School held at the University of Otago in Dunedin. There was at that time a vigorous internal debate on the issue of whether New Zealand's security issues lay entirely in the South Pacific region; or whether their military should be structured and equipped so as to be able to operate with the armed forces of its traditional allies in support of New Zealand's increasingly wide-ranging interests. Nuclear weapons were another 'hot' issue, with the New Zealand government forbidding the visit of any US or UK warships without full assurance that there were no nuclear weapons on board, an assurance that US and UK governments were unwilling to give. I was also invited to speak on nuclear issues to a gathering, at the Department of Foreign Affairs and Trade in Auckland. This included representatives of the anti-nuclear movement. It all went well although at one point I carelessly lapsed into naval jargon by referring to an "NDB". I was asked what on earth that was. I replied that it was a short title for a nuclear anti-submarine depth bomb. I added light-heartedly that in my private life in England it was often in my mind referring to the hunt called the Newcastle and District Beagles.

On hearing this and following the meeting, the charming lady in charge of my programme told me that her neighbour was a keen hunting man and suggested that I might go down to the South Island at the weekend to visit the kennels of the South Canterbury Hounds. I was delighted at this offer and by being invited by the New Zealand Deputy Chief of Naval Staff to stay at his farm. My visit to the South Canterbury Hunt was a great joy for me. The kennel huntsman's wife was from an English hunting family whom I knew. Nearby lived Marshal of the Royal Air Force Lord Elworthy, whose wife had launched and been the sponsor for HMS INTREPID, which I had subsequently commanded. He had been a highly respected Chief of Defence in Britain. I had met him on several other occasions in his role as Governor of Windsor Castle. Also nearby lived a very famous Irish foxhunting man, Thady Ryan. Some of the hounds in the South Canterbury pack had been bred from hounds drafted to New Zealand many years before from my own neighbouring pack in South Devon, the South Pool Harriers. I felt very much at home.

The next day I was invited by my host, the commodore, to go horse riding with him and his son on his farm, which lay in the most beautiful country to the south of Canterbury. It was a glorious day. In one respect his farm resembled my own on Dartmoor, in that the gates were not easy to open. "Don't worry," said my host, "We'll just jump them." The hills were steep and the scenery magnificent. The horses fortunately were very sure-footed. At the end of the ride, my host said that his son, who was riding a young horse, would go round the other way as the gate that we were about to jump was rather formidable. The thought sprang strongly that I would rather go with his son – but I did not want to be chicken. I had not noticed that immediately after landing, we would have to turn sharp right through a small dip to where the cars were waiting for us. My horse jumped the gate clearly – but I didn't; and on landing, found myself half way up the horse's neck. Even though I was confident in the horse's sure-footedness I thought that the right thing to do, whilst I regained my seat, was to avoid the sharp right hand turn and go the long way round. Unfortunately the horse didn't agree, and at that moment he was in charge and I was not. The next thing I knew was that I was being carried to a car. What had happened was that as the horse, not under my control, turned sharp right, my weight fell on my left stirrup leather, which broke and I flew out the 'side door'. Before landing I had collided with a large gatepost that I knocked clean out of the ground with my left shoulder. I was very lucky to survive because I was not wearing a hard hat and had I hit the post head-on I should most likely have been killed.

I slept very little that night and was taken early next morning to see the doctor. He assured me that my collarbone was not broken and that I only had severe bruising. He commented that it made a change for him from rugby injuries. With further good fortune I recovered quickly and was able to play tennis in Sydney three days later before going on to Canberra for discussions about the forthcoming Council on Security Co-operation in the Asia-Pacific, the meeting of which was due to take place in Kuala Lumpur shortly afterwards.

The growth of cohesion amongst the Asian countries presented its problems for Europe. Besides the British, several European countries including the Dutch, the French and the Portuguese, also had a long history of colonial administration in the Asia Pacific region. In representational terms, they did not fit into the new Asian collective structures such as ASEAN. Representation by the European Community was also unsatisfactory, since the EC principle of a rotating presidency, even when acting as a troika, lacked consistency and authority. Thus in 1996, a new informal forum was set up, the East Asian-European Meeting (ASEM). It was first convened in Bangkok in 1996, attended by representatives of thirty-eight European and East Asian countries. A second ASEM meeting at Heads of Government level was held in London in 1998. Tony Blair described its aim as "to make a real difference to our peoples; improving welfare and education of our young peoples; increasing the business links and commerce between us; confronting together the financial turbulence in Asia: and co-operating in our efforts to protect the environment."

Its most recent meeting was in 2006 in Helsinki which approved an agreed Declaration on the future of ASEM[10].

By the time of the handover of the British sovereignty of Hong Kong to China in 1997, the threat by China to the sovereignty of the South China Sea islands had effectively disappeared from the agenda. This helped to provide an opportunity for trying to improve the British relationship with the 'new' China. I was therefore asked to visit Beijing in 1998 to meet with the Vice President of the People's Institute of Foreign Affairs to discuss the creation of a non-governmental forum whose remit would cover the full range of political, economic, security, business and social issues. Such a forum would serve to exchange views on global matters of common interest, to act as a catalyst for action by government and other appropriate bodies, to help establish networks of personal contacts and to encourage the activities of more specialist bilateral subgroups. I was warmly received in the Foreign Ministry and in a number of other non-government institutions to which the British Embassy had arranged visits. There were no subjects, not even Tibet, that were off limits. I had the clear impression that all with whom I spoke were delighted to hear views on international issues, other than those that they regularly heard from the United States.

I found Beijing a fascinating city, so different from my other long-ago experiences of Shanghai and Canton. Times had indeed changed. My hotel, close to Tiananmen Square, was well up to western standards. The square, despite the tragic events there of the cultural revolution, displayed a truly historic and majestic aura. In the city, the roads were now almost as full of motorcars as they were of bicycles, pedicabs and rickshaws. Close at hand were large Chinese emporia selling everything from modern TV sets, digital cameras, and the latest western clothing styles with appropriate western fashion labels. They were packed with Chinese shoppers. Western shoppers were hardly to be seen -

---

[10] *This is available on the Internet*

they were all visiting the Chinese downtown markets, buying the traditional tourist bits and pieces and touristy clothing.

I returned to London with the view that, with careful diplomacy, there was the opportunity for establishing a UK-China non-governmental group, in a similar way to that which led to the founding of the UK-Japan 2000 Group. By that time however, certain difficulties occurring within the Royal Institute, led me to the decision that it was time for me personally to withdraw from what I regarded as an exciting prospect. In the event, no such wide-ranging group has yet emerged, although a considerable number of specialist joint taskforces have now been created - particularly in the fields of climate change and scientific research. Close contacts have also been established between the cities of London and Shanghai on financial matters, co-operation which was underpinned by a naval visit to Shanghai by HMS WESTMINSTER in 2004, only the second UK naval visit to Shanghai in more than fifty years. In the same year, an official visit by Prime Minister Wen Jiabao to London resulted in a long statement of common aims and actions[11].

It is not always appreciated that India is an Asian subcontinent. India first raised itself into my own consciousness when my uncle, Eric Marriott, returned to England having retired from the Indian Police. I was seven years old. He came to stay with us at Redland Park, Bristol. The basement of our house was full of his luggage – great big cabin trunks with prominent labels "NOT WANTED ON VOYAGE" – a well used gun case containing his two sporting rifles – a packing case containing his sporting trophies. One of these was a leopard skin which we draped over the back of the settee in our morning room. It was all very exciting and it was about India.

In 1945, as a naval midshipman, the first foreign soil on which I set foot was in India, at Bombay. In 1981 on my round-the-world farewell as the Commander-in-Chief of the Fleet, my last port of call was Bombay, having had the prior privilege in Delhi of sitting-

---

[11] *Internet. "UK China relations"*

in at a meeting of the Indian Naval Board. It was a remarkable experience as it reminded me all too clearly of one of our own Admiralty Board meetings in London. Here was the Indian Navy displaying its own proud heritage as an offspring of the Royal Navy. Having moved on to spend the next day visiting the Indian naval dockyard at Bombay, which maintained both former British and Russian warships, I had another exciting experience at the airport. The official from the High Commission who accompanied me in my car to the airport on completion of my day's programme was able, most helpfully, to short circuit the horrendous queues at the check-in desks and the departure lounges. He then insisted that the car would take me to the foot of the steps of my BA Flight. This aircraft was parked among a large number of other aircraft somewhere on the departure apron - but where? It was a wet and drizzly night with low visibility, and at one moment I was convinced that we were driving on one of the runways. The driver's tactic was to drive close to the rear steps of each successive aircraft, and lowering his window, shout at the top of his voice "London?" When one reply came back, "No. Moscow," I began to get a little concerned. In due course we thankfully came to an aircraft that I recognised to be in BA colours and from which echoed the cry, "Yes – London".

Ten years later I was delighted to be invited to stop off at New Delhi on my return home from Japan so as to address the Indian Senior Defence College and attend an international conference on "Regional Co-operation in Maritime Affairs". Some years later, I was again in Delhi for a conference on "An Indian Ocean Community", a concept running in parallel with another slow moving initiative for a "South Asian Area of Regional Co-operation" (SAARC). Such 'visions' at least had the virtue of improving some of the trickier and potentially dangerous bilateral political disputes within the region. I was particularly struck by the Indian concerns as to China's presence on her northern border and particularly in relation to Tibet. This was matched amongst the naval community by the unstable situation in Burma. The danger that was foreseen there was that either Russia or China would persuade Rangoon to offer naval base facilities, so allowing the establishment of a prospectively hostile naval presence in the Eastern Indian Ocean. A threat to the hegemony of the Indian Navy in any part of the Indian Ocean was of major concern.

I was particularly grateful for an opportunity in the margins of the conference to meet and discuss various issues with the Italian born Mrs Indira Ghandi, with whom I was greatly impressed. I also had the privilege of addressing the National Defence College and the Indian Defence Studies Association. Today, the emergence of India and China, both with their massive internal problems, as growing global economic players, greatly complicates the future global and Asian security balance. But that is a matter for my final chapter.

Chapter 9

The 21st Century, Terrorism and the Future

"Old sailors never die, they just stop pulling on the sheets."
                                                                    Anon

The previous chapters of this trilogy have described events of the past, beginning in Book 1 in the sixteenth century (*"From Greenland's Icy Shores"*); Book 2 (*"Life on the Ocean Waves"*) begins in 1941 when I joined the Navy and finishes at the end of my sea going career in the late 1970's. In Book 3, I have so far described the events of my more senior life from then until the close of my professionally active life at the turn of the last century. This final chapter turns to the situation following the dramatic changes in the world order of a new century after the attack on New York and other US targets in September 2001, and takes a brief look into some of the wider issues of the future of international defence and security.

Immediately following the attack on the twin towers, US President George Bush declared that this was not merely an act of international terrorism, it was "an act of war" and declared "War on Terror". The use of these two terms, war and terror, whose characteristics are so very different, as an expression at that time is excusable, but it has since caused serious confusion. The challenge of war is fundamentally different from that of terrorism. In war you have a readily identifiable enemy - this is not so in dealing with terrorism. Wars have finite territorial boundaries - terrorism does not. Wars have a finite beginning and end. This is not so with terrorism. Sinn Fein and the Northern Ireland problem have provided for Britain in the post World War II years a salutary lesson in terrorism, terrorism based almost entirely on religious bigotry. The battle has been fought on both sides with armed force. On neither side has it prevailed. Modern terrorism will not be defeated by twenty-first century warfare.

The definition of 'War' in the Oxford Dictionary occupies no less than eight column inches. It centres on the idea that war is "conducted between nations by force", although It accepts the much more limited definition of "hostility between persons". These definitions are of course open to wide interpretation. We are all familiar with the expressions cold war and hot war. Nevertheless it is widely accepted that the fundamentals of war involve a dispute between nations and states that involves the use of armed force. Countries do not initiate war if they are not confident of winning. The perception of war by individuals and therefore by the leaders of states is strongly influenced by personal experience. For my father, his experiences of World War I in France were of the carnage and appalling conditions of the long war on the western front. For me, I always have in the back of my mind the advice of an unknown colleague given to me when, at the age of seventeen, I went on my first operational sortie in World War II, in which not a lot really happened, that "war is ninety-five percent boredom – and five percent sheer terror".

The causes of war were generally seen as a dispute over the 'ownership' of territory. In practice they were far more complex. In the nineteenth century in Germany there were many disputes over the boundaries of the new German republic. One of these concerned the territories of Schleswig Holstein. Gladstone's reported statement in the British parliament on this issue is indicative. *"There are only three people who fully understood the Schleswig Holstein problem. One was the Kaiser and he is dead. The other was an official in the Foreign Office and he went mad. The other was me and I have forgotten".*

Much more recently there was the 1980 Iran-Iraq war. This was seen by many in the western world as "a war between two four-letter countries",the differences between the two which were neither known nor understood. Furthermore, there was no clear understanding of what the war was all about. I myself was in a position of needing a fast learning process – although my dominant memory of that period is of the intelligence on the progress of the war on the battlefield which came to me from the

United States in my role as Commander-in-Chief of the Fleet. It provided me with a new understanding of the degree of sophistication of the US satellite intelligence gathering capability in land warfare.

Unlike terrorism, the characteristics of war differ between the three armed services. For those in the army, war at its lowest level inevitably involves personal conflict between one person and another, the outcome of which is probably that either you get killed or he does. For the Navy the personal perception of war is different, man does not fight man – ship fights ship. You may spend your morning in making every effort to sink an opposing ship – and then, if successful, you may spend the rest of the day trying to rescue its survivors from the sea. For the Air Force, the personal concept of war is again very different. It is only a very few, the aircrew, who are normally ever in direct contact with the enemy. It is this reality that makes the idea of having a single service, rather than three services working in very close co-operation, an idea whose time has *not* come; and probably never will. This aspect of the personal experience of war, or the lack of it, greatly affects the attitude of those in political authority. In Britain and also in America, there are now very few in positions of political authority with personal experience of the conditions of war. We are all now learning how best to face the challenges of international terrorism.

The character of war has inevitably changed with time, driven by the development of new weaponry. World War I was basically fought between armies. Civilian populations other than those on the battlefield were not directly involved. In World War II, the battlefield was extended to civilian populations by the use of air power, which was used effectively to destroy cities like Coventry, Dresden and Hamburg. The advent of nuclear weapons further expanded the vulnerability of civilian populations as was demonstrated at Hiroshima and Nagasaki. The cold war in Europe, however, confirmed a new concept of war which threatened both our way of life and our territorial integrity. It was not fought between armed forces, but entailed a bitter struggle between political and sociological ideologies, those of democracy and communism. Both sides were backed by a vast military-warfighting potential that was only restrained by the deterrent capability of increasingly powerful nuclear weapons.

With the ending of the cold war, and the resulting reduction in the extent of the global nuclear threat, I had hopes that the Nuclear Non-Proliferation Treaty would lead towards the global acceptance that nuclear weapons would further lead to a change in our global thinking about the use of armed force as an effective agent for achieving political, economic or ideological change. As Mr Gorbachev himself phrased it, "one country's security cannot be obtained at the price of the insecurity of another". Clearly, in the nuclear field, this has not influenced the conduct of either the Iranian or North Korean governments. Nor has the British government's intended retention and modernisation of its strategic "Trident" arsenal been entirely helpful in this respect.

The ending of the cold war introduced a new factor at the international level which was the growth of what became known as "non-state actors". Some non-state actors were entirely peaceful and broadly beneficial to mankind – such as Greenpeace and Amnesty International. At the other end of the spectrum lay groups based on religious and ideological beliefs causing conflict both between states and within states, as in Afghanistan, and Central Asia where tribal affiliations are strong. Such tribal conflicts are prevalent throughout the world, in Spain, in Sri Lanka, in Burma, and throughout the African continent. My own failure to realise that the collapse of communism was not going to lead to a kinder or more peaceful world was largely due to an underestimation of the degree to which such differences could lead to acts of international terrorism, sometimes falling not far short of outright war.

The Oxford Dictionary defines a terrorist as "a person attempting to further his view or trying to rule by subversive intimidation". In historical terms, man has from his earliest days sought to defend himself, his family and his way of life. Threats to his aspirations, other than from nature, came from other human beings with different ideas. Our forbears therefore armed themselves with weapons and joined a tribe sharing, common values, which could by its collective efforts better provide for the *security* of the individual and of the tribe. In due course there developed the Nation State which itself raised armed forces for the purpose of defending its citizens and promoting the states way of life. As the well-known quotation from Clausewitz reminds us, *war* became an extension of diplomacy by other means. Anyone who was involved in the higher levels of NATO during the cold war is well aware of the deep tensions that from time to time arose between the need for diplomacy and political cohesion, and the requirements of military doctrine.

Terrorism was not unknown during the cold war – for instance the 1972 attack on Israeli athletes at the Munich Olympic Games. With the ending of the cold war, these conflicts were fuelled by the increased availability of the weapons of individual conflict – modern high performance small arms, rocket propelled grenades and small explosive devices. Their spread was worldwide and often aimed at United States interests, such as the Libya sponsored Lockerbie air disaster, the attacks on US embassies in Africa, the attack on a US Marine barracks in Lebanon and the 1993 attack on the World Trade Centre in New York. They thus inevitably involved other countries.

There did not seem to be any coherent rationale that linked these events other than as a protest against American domination of the free world's international political and economic agenda. However, America was not slow to respond with measures of a strongly military nature as in the case of Libya, and Colonel Gadaffi's support for international terrorism. In 1986, the American Sixth Fleet launched a series of air attacks on Libyan territory. Such action was perceived by many Europeans as dangerously over reactive. In an interview with Newsweek in New York in May 1986, when asked to review the European reaction to the American air attacks, I said, *"Europeans find it hard to see terrorism as an act of war. They see it as a challenge to society, not a threat to national security."*

It is argued that the creation of Muslim anti-western extremism, whether in the Middle East or in South East Asia has been a result of western, and particularly American, attempts to impose upon others western concepts of governance and civil order which are inimical to their culture. In that case, then we must consider to what extent we may now be building a similar reaction of extremism amongst African countries, not based on ideological grounds, but on grounds of poverty and disease, reinforced by the ravages of climate change. This situation is already apparent in the area of the Sudan and the Horn of Africa.

It was the 9/11 attack on the twin towers that represented, not least in terms of the death roll, a major escalation and sophistication in terrorist activity. It brought to the public attention the organisation of Al Qaeda, headed by Osama bin Laden as its self-appointed leader. Al Qaeda's origin lay in the jihadist organisations which had opposed Soviet intervention in Afghanistan and which in 1989 led to the withdrawal of Russian forces. It is understandable, bearing in mind American experience of Pearl Harbour, that President Bush should have described this as an "act of war" – a statement echoed by certain British and European political leaders who ought to have known better. This has led through various twists and turns in the development of international actions, to the situation in which the US, the UK and NATO found themselves in 2006 in Iraq and Afghanistan. I well remember my own reaction as I watched the destruction of the twin towers live on television in my home – it was that the world would never be the same again.

The American response to 9/11, supported by the United Nations, was swift. On the 7th of October 2001 the US launched military operations in Afghanistan against its Taliban government that was held responsible for harbouring Bin Laden and his Al Qaeda movement. Such military action, led by American forces, many of whom were later based in the territories of the former southern states of the Soviet Union, was supported by a broad coalition of international forces. The Taliban forces were defeated and the government, which had been in power since 1996, was deposed.

Steps were taken to establish a new democratically elected Afghani Government.

A year later, the US announced its government's decision to abandon the strategy of deterrence and to substitute one of pre-emption[12]. This fundamental strategic change was made without effective public policy or academic debate in the US or elsewhere. This policy was reaffirmed in March 2006. It can be argued, and I myself would do so, that the cause of stability in the international system was thereby potentially undermined.

The heart of the wider problem, that of the rise of international terrorism, soon turned to Iraq and its ruler Saddam Hussein. The 1995 attack by Iraq on Kuwait was clearly an act of war ostensibly aimed at resolving an issue of ownership of the key oil fields that straddled the international accepted border between Iraq and Kuwait. The international response, led by the United States, was correct and decisive. Whether the action should have been continued after Iraqi forces had been cleared from Kuwait is one that will continue to be a matter of dispute. My own opinion at the time was that the decision was correct - not least on the grounds that Saddam Hussein's own troops would have displayed a far greater order of effectiveness in defending their home territory. This also would have had further consequential penalties to the Iraqi civil population.

Nevertheless it inevitably coloured American views on Iraq and its leadership when further concerns were raised by their apparent quest for nuclear weapons. The saga of the events leading up to the US-led invasion of Iraq in March 2003 presents a picture of confusion. In the United States the necessity for war was presented to congress and the American people both as the failure of the Iraqi government to comply with UN resolutions and the need for regime change, Saddam Hussein being seen as a modern day Hitler.

---

[12] *US National Security Strategy. Sept. 20, 2002*

On the first count, such action is clearly contrary to the charter of the United Nations in that Article 2 (4) commits its members to *"refrain in their international relations from the threat or use of force against the territorial integrity or the political independence of any state or in any other manner inconsistent with the Purposes of the United Nations"*. In the United Nations Security Council, a Resolution was based on the multiple rejections by Iraq of previous Security Council Resolutions. However, Article 6 of the UN Charter states that, *"a member of the United Nations which has consistently violated the principles contained in the present charter may be expelled from the Organisation by the General Assembly upon the recommendation of the Security Council"*. It says nothing about the use of force to ensure compliance. In Britain the principal reason for the invasion was the alleged direct threat presented to the United Kingdom by Iraqi nuclear weapons – which, it was subsequently admitted, did not exist.

Whatever the reason, right or wrong, for initiating war on Iraq with the objective of regime change, it clearly gave little or no consideration as to the likely outcome in terms of the internal polity of Iraq. There was apparently nobody at the head of government to ask the vital question, "And what happens then?" The idea that the Shia would seek accommodation with the Sunni in some form of democratic union can be said only to have been born out of ignorance. The Shia did not want democracy – they wanted revenge. The Kurds wanted only autonomy. The heavy damage that the war caused on the country's infrastructure, electric power, water, communications was perhaps an affordable cost if the war was to be short and brutal – as the American military concept of 'shock and awe' was. However, the destruction of the structure of internal administration including the organs of order, the police and the army, essentially guaranteed that the conclusion of the war-fighting phase would have the inevitable result of chaos.

That the British cabinet was prepared to endorse the flawed decision by Tony Blair to go to war is one of the greatest ever failures of cabinet responsibility at the senior cabinet level. Only Robin Cook had the guts to express his opposition in terms of resignation. It is sad that he is no longer alive today to understand how right he was. Not only was the cabinet's failure to understand the fragility of Tony Blair's decision for war, it was also their failure to understand that the British government's rationale for war had failed to convince a very large proportion of the British public as demonstrated by their march against the Iraq war attended by over one million people.

The recent outcome of the American mid-term elections have served to bring into the public domain more information about the Bush administration's rationale for Iraqi regime change, the American approach to the United Nations and the sequence of events leading to Tony Blair's complete acceptance of the American position. This in turn may loosen the British Labour government's refusal to undertake a fundamental review of the Prime Minister's decision to support President Bush's commitment to war – and the appalling misjudgement, perpetrated with the apparent agreement of the intelligence community, that Iraq presented a nuclear threat to the United Kingdom. To anyone who was involved in the practices of posing a realistic nuclear threat to an opposing government, this was clearly a nonsense, the result of which has already been a major factor in shaping the world of the early twenty-first century.

It is now apparent that whilst the twentieth century was one in which war in its well-understood nature involving conflict between nations over the domination of foreign and sovereign territories, the twenty-first century conflict is between and within ideologies and not between nation states. Such conflict cannot be resolved by military action. A fundamental error in the philosophy of America's war on terror is the belief that democratic government can be imposed by the outcome of military action in countries that have no experience or collective memory of what is meant by democracy. Indeed, what do we ourselves mean by "democratic" government? In the last general election in Britain, more people voted for the Conservative party than for the Labour party – yet a Labour government was returned.

In Iraq, following the subsequent disastrous outcome of the US-led invasion, it seems very unlikely that any government that could be fairly described as 'a working democracy' can be established in Baghdad in the near future. The reality is that the situation in Iraq will merely add one further dimension to the fundamental instability of the Middle East region. In Afghanistan, the situation that has unfolded makes it equally unlikely that a stable internal democracy will prevail for a long time, beset as it is by deep tribal divisions in which democracy is neither understood, nor has it before been practised. Its many local warlords, generously financed through international drug trafficking, are unlikely to give up their fiefdoms willingly to a central government in Kabul. The history of previous wars of intervention in Afghanistan, both British and Russian, is certainly not a harbinger for success. The present commitment of troops from NATO countries to the region is clearly not popular amongst the electorates of a number of European countries, not least in Britain. This is aggravated not only by casualties in a vicious war against the Taliban but also by President Bush's failed policies towards Iraq. Some of NATO's Afghanistan commitments expire in 2008 and their renewal must be politically uncertain.

In the wider context of the Middle East, conflict centres both around the religious divide between Shia and Sunni Muslims within and between countries, and the Israeli-Palestinian dispute. These conflicts have produced a high degree of internal and regional instability which condition has been made worse by the US led invasion of Iraq. The continuing chaos in the Middle East of a religious, social, ethnic and economic nature seems likely to raise the levels of internal military conflict and encourage the export of terrorist activities. Where this may lead seems likely to be on the international agenda for a long time to come.

The problem that we are now left with is where do we go from here both in Iraq and Afghanistan in the short term. If we accept the stated view of the head of MI5, that the threat of international terrorism in this country is both real, sustained and likely to remain so for a generation, then the idea that British troops should continue to be deployed in the Middle East along what has been termed by President Bush "the axis of terrorism" is unlikely to command public support. The issue therefore remains how quickly and under what least damaging context can such withdrawal be conducted.

In a recent conversation about the rationale for NATO's military involvement in Afghanistan, a former British minister and leader in the field of international security, told me that when seeking additional troop levels to reinforce NATO's commitment to Afghanistan, he was asked by a European government leader how she should explain to her people why NATO was involved in a war in Afghanistan. He had replied that the answer was simple, "If we do not go to Afghanistan, Afghanistan will come to us." I find this a typical political sound bite and have been unable to fathom what it actually means, especially given the existing failure to control overseas migration into Britain and the clear failure of the policy of multi-culturism, failures that need urgently to be addressed.

Failure in Afghanistan would seem almost certainly to reopen the question that has dogged the NATO debate since the end of the cold war – "What is NATO for?" In 1990, speaking in my valedictory address to the Royal Institute of International Affairs, I argued that NATO had outlived its usefulness and should "remain in being only as long as necessary to create the conditions that would allow it to be dissolved.[13]" In 1998, a powerful group of most senior former British ministers, ambassadors and military defence chiefs expressed their public opposition to plans to expand NATO to include countries from central and eastern Europe[14].

---

[13] *The Independent 19th December 1990*
[14] *Daily telegraph 6th May 1998*

Despite the well handled programmes such as NATO's Partners for Peace (PfP) [15], and the progressive integration of former East European countries into the European Union, recent developments in the Putin administration in Russia clearly indicate much residual resentment of what is seen as the continuing encirclement of the former Soviet Union by its previous enemies, as had been widely forecast.

However, the question of "What is NATO now for?" was overtaken by the events of the first Gulf war and the Balkan wars in the period 1990-1999 when NATO, after long and complex negotiations involving the United Nations, transformed its former Treaty commitment to self-defence against attack within a designated European area, to the authorisation of out of area peace keeping and peace enforcement operations. This resulted in the use of NATO air power against the Bosnian Serbs in 1993 and in the Serbian-Kosovo conflict in 1999[16]. NATO has thus become a 'come in handy' transatlantic military organisation, with air, sea and land capabilities, backed by intelligence, planning, logistic, command and communication facilities, for the conduct of *warfare*. It has little to do directly with solving the basic threats to *security*, as are now represented by ideological dogmatism being perpetrated by Muslim extremists.

In 2007, it has become easier to define what NATO should *not* be for, rather than what it *is* for. It should not be for the support of US military adventures in the Middle East nor as a base for the deployment in Europe of US anti-ballistic missile capability to defend the United States from nuclear missile threats from US defined "rogue states". Nor do I believe it can be effective by taking military action against countries seen as the home of international terrorist activities. However, if NATO were no longer to be the basis for transatlantic defence co-operation, what then is to be the basis for defence co-operation within the growing

---

[15] *Google "The Partnership for Peace" May 2007*
[16] *Google "NATO Air attacks in the Balkans"*

European Union, spreading from the eastern shores of the Baltic to the eastern shores of the Mediterranean and Black Sea?

There are of course various forms of defence co-operation. Amongst the most valuable of these is European collaboration in defence procurement, leading to weapon and logistic standardisation and compatible operational capability. This is an area that the newly established EU Development Agency is addressing. There is also the recent establishment, under the banner of the EU Common Foreign and Security Policy (CFSP), of an EU military operations centre and EU Battle Groups. Whilst this does not constitute a direct challenge to NATO, there is at each turn of the EU 'screw', a price to be paid in terms of the strength and closeness of the transatlantic relationship

The US-European relationship has been a central political and military condition of Atlantic security throughout the two world wars of the last century. Within this transatlantic relationship there is no field more important than that of defence and security policy. However, American action in Iraq and EU assertiveness in this field has made future prospects for close co-operation in foreign and security policy increasingly uncertain. Even within the European Union, the development of CFSP is a fundamentally difficult task, not least because of differing interpretations of defence and security. But more fundamentally, the concept of a search for a meaningful common foreign policy between twenty-seven countries, so deeply divided by geography, history, political, economic and religious background, becomes a 'mission impossible'. The creation of an EU Foreign Minister (or High Representative) is no more than the appointment of 'an emperor without any clothes'. Since it is widely accepted that defence policy has to be the servant of foreign policy, this does not bode well for cohesion in the operational aspects of any EU common security policy.

Indeed, the likely final outcome of the 2007 negotiations to reform the very basis of the EU's structure, in the form of a new 'mini-treaty' to replace the formerly proposed EU Constitution, is still uncertain. In Britain there is widespread opposition to any further transfer of national sovereignty to Brussels. If the new mini-treaty is seen to be no more than a pale reflection of the previously rejected constitution, then such a more powerful EU Government would represent for very many people in Britain "a government too far". At a time when there is widespread criticism of the performance of the British parliamentary system, there is also deep concern that the European parliament with representatives of twenty-seven countries can never be more than a very expensive and ineffective talking shop. There is similar concern about the effective performance of the European Commission representing twenty-seven national governments.

In the present circumstances, despite the claim that previous changes to the EU treaty had not called for a referendum, a refusal by the British Government to call for a referendum on the continued acceptability of the new mini-treaty could only be seen as an act of supreme political cowardice. In defence of the principles of our freedoms, for which so many of our forbears have fought and given their lives in two world wars, there would be a strong case for a national campaign of civil disobedience to force such a referendum.

With the end of the cold war, the ideological and territorial threat to Britain and Western Europe has disappeared over the horizon. This is not to say that Russia has become a comfortable neighbour for Western Europe – nor that we shall no longer have to fear territorial or resource challenges from that or other quarters. Some recent Putin utterances have, however, been interpreted as threatening a return to the cold war. I do not believe this to be so. Russia has too many international economic interests at stake to risk warfare, hot or cold.

Nevertheless, many British people still feel that their life style is threatened. The newly perceived threats arise through racial tensions, terrorism, social change, global warming, immigration, and the overbearing burden of ever increasing government regulation. These are all threats to their security – but their solution does not lie in war fighting.

The threat of communism has now been replaced by the challenge of Muslim extremism. Extremism, whether in the racial or religious field, will not be defeated on the battlefield. It is not confined to the Middle East but at present flourishes there. It has therefore to be countered at the international level, by measures of a political, economic and societal nature, which may involve nation building and the rescue of failed states. Within Britain, government policies on multi-culturalism, the lack of effective immigration controls and our military involvement internally in Iraq and Afghanistan have helped to create a situation of deep discomfort which is unlikely to be speedily resolved. This will, however, require very close co-operation between all national and international security agencies.

The wider question that faces Britain is that of its future defence policy. In an age of extremism that challenges the stability of our society, do we still need to maintain a worldwide capability for war fighting; and if we do, can we afford it at an appropriate level of capability? The simple answer is that as a permanent member of the United Nations we have a responsibility for global stability and thus for an appropriate military capability to sustain it. As a leading member of NATO, we carry a similar responsibility within Europe – although this has now been extended to Afghanistan; where the original concept of military measures to assist in nation building (soft power) and thus combat international terrorism, has turned into open warfare (hard power) against the Taliban.

Former Prime Minister Tony Blair addressed this issue in an interesting speech made onboard HMS Albion in Plymouth on the 12th of January 2007[17]. He expressed the problem thus, "There is a case for Britain in the early twenty-first century with its imperial strength behind it, to slip graciously into a different role. We become the leaders in the fight against climate change, against global poverty, for peace and reconciliation; and we leave the demonstration of hard power to others. I do not share that case but there is quite a large part of public opinion that does."

---

[17] *RUSI Journal of February 2007*

He later added, "Terrorism cannot be defeated by military means alone. But it cannot be defeated without it."

Two key factors seem likely to govern the approach of British people. Firstly as an island nation with limited remaining energy assets – Britain's coal assets have now reached the limit of exploitation - the supply of oil and gas in the North Sea is continuing to diminish - what capabilities of a military nature might be required to maintain access to external energy sources?

A second deciding factor in questions of war and security will rest on the developing shape of the world. This is likely to follow the pattern of economic and trade development, as well as measures of national wealth. We live in an age of increasing globalism for the conduct of international trade and investment. Whilst it would be ideal for trading relationships between countries in and between trading blocs to be governed by clear international rules, the very difficult and slow progress made in negotiations of the World Trading Organisation (WTO) do not provide a basis for optimism. Similarly interbloc negotiations (USA and EU) do not offer optimism either.

The present principal world trading groups are the EU, MERCOSUR (the Latin American grouping,), APEC (the Asia Pacific Economic Community), the USA, China and Japan; and at present in the energy field, Russia. The question to be addressed is whether the formation of other such economic powerhouses will lead to more or less trade friction and thus to greater or less international stability. It can be argued that a world consisting of large trading blocs will lead to less trade friction. In counterpoint it can be argued that in areas of very high national importance (e.g. energy supplies) where agreement cannot be reached, recourse to military action to safeguard national interests is more likely to be an option. The growth of global investment could lead to intriguing possibilities for cyber war. We must also consider the reverse situation in which major economic blocs give way to smaller groupings of common economic interest. In this case military action may still occur but its nature would be on a much smaller scale.

An alternative picture of future global structure can be based not on economic interests but on those of religious and cultural conflict. Such conflict has provided the basis for long and bitter wars throughout the centuries – that of Genghis Khan and his attempted domination of early western culture to that for the Middle East and Western Europe - the Crusades which pitched the Christian faith against the infidels of the Middle East - the religious wars of the fifteenth and sixteenth centuries in central Europe between the adherents to the Church of Rome and those of the protestant faith – and today between the Christian and extremist Muslim factions. Such conflicts, particularly in Africa may be based on tribal considerations – such as Rwanda. They may similarly be based on internal political, economic and social factors, as in Zimbabwe today. In the area of the Far East, the religious divide between the Muslim countries of southeast Asia and particularly Indonesia, and the Confucian beliefs which still underpin a very large proportion of China's enormous population, and the Shintoist beliefs of northeast Asia and particularly Japan, provide ample grounds for conflict.

What then is the future? As Winston Churchill was once said to have remarked –*"Forecasting is always difficult – and particularly in the future".* In my final fling of "Admiral Jim" I do not intend to fall into this forecasting trap. I shall however attempt to address what might be some of possible areas of international conflict and to set certain hypothetical scenarios which Britain may have to address, and ask the question "And what If ...?"

What if, as a result of actions taken against Iran in the context of her government's aspirations, the Iranians closed the straights of Hermuz, the entrance into the Gulf, by mining and shore-based anti-ship missiles?

What if America shifts the focus of its defence and security interests from the Atlantic to the Pacific?

What if President Musharrif of Pakistan is deposed and, after a period of widespread internal conflict, a fundamentalist Muslim government comes to power?

<u>What if</u> a future Argentine government decides to have another go at taking possession of the Falkland Islands, having first taken out the Mount Pleasant airfield, thus denying Britain the option of rapid re-enforcement?

<u>What if</u>, following an unwise announcement by the President of Taiwan about the island's independence from China, China launches an assault on the island; the US responds with armed force as it is required by treaty to do; the US asks for international support, and particularly from Britain?

<u>What if</u>, as a result of internal political and economic strife in Indonesia, the Indonesian government attacks Brunei in order to take over the wealth of the Seria oilfields?

<u>What if</u> the North Korean state collapses, resulting in renewed fighting in the Korean peninsular involving Chinese and South Korean Forces?

<u>What if</u> the Tamil problem in Sri Lanka starts to involve India more closely, leading to intervention by another power?

<u>What if</u> China and Russia were to form an anti-capitalist alliance against the West?

<u>What if</u>, due to rising sea levels in the Pacific as a result of global warming, the resettlement of their populations became a cause of hostilities, possibly involving European countries?

<u>What if</u> growing insurrection in Myanmar (Burma), leads China to establish a naval presence in the Indian Ocean, based in Rangoon, a move that would likely to be strongly contested by India?

<u>What if</u> growing ethnic and religious divisions in Sinkiang (the westernmost province of China) should lead to conflict within China, Russia and the central Asian republics?

Such a sequence of "what ifs" could be extended almost ad infinitum, perhaps with increasing improbability; and the reaction "what has that got to do with Britain?" I use it to illustrate what a potentially unstable situation in which the world has to live when the avoidance of risk by one may offer an opportunity to another.

This then is for me the compelling need for Britain to maintain a global military reach, in helping to maintain global stability and to lead the global struggle against extremism.

As an Island nation, Britain still depends on the freedom of the seas and their global highways. The International Maritime Organisation (IMO) based in London, one of the most effective UN Agencies, is concerned with the safety and security of international shipping and the world's oceans. It is estimated that over 90% of world trade is still being carried by sea. During the decade 1990 – 2000, world sea-borne trade grew by some 20%, a rate of rise that shows no sign of declining. In the same period, the number of operational ships in the Royal Navy and its manpower strength fell by about the same percentage; although the navy's amphibious support capability was being strengthened.

I will not however, from the depth of my armchair, fall into the error of trying to finish by designing the future Fleet. Suffice it to say that (a) The future capability of the fleet must lie with the planned two new aircraft carriers to operate in support of our amphibious capability afloat and ashore. (b) Surface escorts are vulnerable to air attack as was again shown in the Falklands war. The increasing sophistication of their weaponry also makes them extremely expensive. There thus appears to be a good case for returning to the quantity/quality argument –with John Fieldhouse's remark to me as CINC Fleet, at the conclusion of one of our many discussions on the issue some twenty five years ago, ringing in my ears. He said "Jim, in any balancing of quantity versus quality, quality must win – providing you have enough of it". (c) The increasing capability of both short range and long range air launched weapons also points to a re-evaluation of the surface ship – submarine balance in the fleet. (d) Whatever is done, there will be no lack of those to say later "you got it wrong, chum".

EPILOGUE

I close with a poem written by one of my grand-daughters, then aged eleven.

I pick up the crusted pen.
Where webs have invaded its peace,
The dusted paper sits there – patient
Not touched in years.

I slowly write my feelings.
The soul of my pen is still there,
Never will it be taken away
The heart of the paper lives on.

Never will they die.
But live in peace where they are.
Left alone in the old misted attic.
Their hearts will shine and make you warm.
Their souls will make you laugh and smile.
They will never die but live on.

Hattie Barnard

Homestead Farm
Houghton,
Stockbridge,
HANTS SO20 6LG

July 2007

I dedicate this trilogy to all my family, and to the fortitude and faith of those that went before us over several centuries.

JE
July 2007

The Author

Sir James (Jim) Eberle was born in Bristol on the 31st of May 1927. He entered the Royal Naval College, Dartmouth in 1941, and went to sea on operational service in mid 1944. He first served in motor gunboats in the English Channel, and subsequently in the Indian Ocean and the British Pacific Fleet. At the end of World War II, he was serving in HMS Belfast that was part of the first US-British Task Force to enter Shanghai. He served in HMS Cossack in the Far East from 1947 to 1949; and again in HMS Belfast as the Second Gunnery Officer during the later stages of the Korean War. He specialised in naval gunnery and was deeply involved in the development of the early naval surface-to-air guided weapons.

After early advancement to Commander and Captain, and a period of study as a Defence Fellow at University College, Oxford, he was selected for promotion to Rear Admiral in 1971, one of the three youngest British admirals of the twentieth century.

His Flag Rank appointments included the Flag Officer Sea Training, Flag Officer Carriers and Amphibious Ships, NATO Commander of the UK Atlantic Strike Group; and a member of Naval Board of the Defence Council as Chief of Fleet Support. In 1979, he took over command of the British Fleet, and as NATO Commander in Chief of the Eastern Atlantic and Allied Commander-in-Chief Channel. Following his Fleet Command, he served as Commander-in-Chief of the Naval Home Command during the Falkland war, prior to his retirement from active service in 1983.

In 1984, he was appointed Director of the Royal Institute of International Affairs, a post he held until 1991. In this position he established high-level contacts with many other countries within Western Europe, and also with Russia, Argentina and Japan.

Sir James was awarded the Knight Grand Cross of the Order of the Bath in 1978. His banner, based on a Moravian shield of the seventeenth century, is hung in St George's Chapel of

The Admiral receives his honorary degree at Bristol University

The Admiral with his hounds at the Royal Naval College Dartmouth

Westminster Abbey. He has served as Vice Admiral of the United Kingdom and as ADC to Her Majesty the Queen. He was granted the honorary position of Admiral in the Texan and Georgian navies.

He is a Freeman of the City of London (1991) and of the City of Bristol (1947) He holds an Honorary Doctorate of Laws at Bristol University (1989) and an Honorary Degree of Doctor of Letters at Sussex University (1992). He was a member of the Vice Chancellor of Exeter University's Advisory Board for Development (1993). He was Chairman of the Council of Clifton College (1984-1994). He was for many years Chairman of the naval professional journal, the Naval Review. He has strong countryside interests having farmed on Dartmoor. He is a Board member of the Countryside Alliance. He has been a Master of the Britannia Beagles at the RN College Dartmouth for fifty years. He played tennis for the Royal Navy for some thirty years and is a member of the All England Lawn Tennis Club at Wimbledon.

He has published three other books – "British Space Policy and International Collaboration" (1987), in conjunction with Dr Helen Wallace (Chatham House Paper no 42) – "Jim. First of the Pack" (1982) a centenary history of the Royal Navy's Britannia Beagles. – and "Management in the Armed Forces" in conjunction with Air Vice Marshal John Downey.